LEGACY

THE HISTORY OF SEPARATELY MANAGED ACCOUNTS

SYDNEY LeBLANC

This book is available at a special discount when ordered in bulk quantities. For information, contact The Money Management Institute at (202) 347-3858 or www.moneyinstitute.com.

This publication is designed to provide accurate and authoritative information in regard to the subject matter covered. It is sold with the understanding that the publisher and author are not engaged in rendering legal, accounting, or other professional services. If legal advice or other expert assistance is required, the services of a competent professional should be sought.

ISBN 0-9721958-0-7

Printed in the United States of America by Monroe Litho, Rochester, New York
Second printing July 2003

LEGACY

THE HISTORY OF SEPARATELY MANAGED ACCOUNTS

In Memory of James Lockwood, 1917–1994

He was a war hero, an industry visionary, and a kind and selfless mentor. The memorable stories about the life and times of consulting pioneer James Lockwood are too numerous to all be included in this book, but they are intrinsically linked to the history of managed accounts. Consultants, advisors, brokers and money managers who knew and worked with Jim loved and respected him. Their words of admiration and anecdotes about the man who "embraced life," and worked tirelessly for his clients, are celebrated throughout this text.

One can't help but wonder if, when Jim Lockwood developed and promoted his concept of serving clients' needs on an institutional caliber level, he realized his legacy would prove to be so far-reaching. Almost 40 years ago, he questioned the validity and value of charging commissions instead of fees. The importance of sitting on the same side of the table with clients, the elimination of potential conflicts of interest, the value of consulting and the investment process, and the opportunity for the individual investor to receive the same quality of investment management as Fortune 500 companies were paramount to Jim.

Today, four decades later, thousands of his fellow advisors breathe life into these principles on a daily basis. As friend and colleague John Ellis likes to say, "I'm sure Jim is looking down on all this, smiling, and toasting us with a glass of Corton-Charlemagne, his favorite white burgundy wine." It is fitting we dedicate this book to Jim Lockwood and other pioneers who had the courage to challenge the conventional financial trade mindset and help revolutionize an entire industry.

Thank you, Jim, on behalf of your friends, colleagues, and those of us who never knew you. Stronger than ever, your legacy endures.

— SYDNEY LEBLANC

TABLE OF CONTENTS

Appropriate timing.... Not the kind that predicts the rise and fall of the equity and fixed income markets, but the kind that recognizes changes in the investment environment and is always rewarded by the financial industry.

This became increasingly evident in the late 1960s and early 1970s at a time when three million shares traded on the New York Stock Exchange was considered a high volume day. Concurrently, numerous unprecedented regulatory changes occurred that changed the very fabric of the investment industry. Only a few industry leaders could envision how future generations of investors would integrate these changes.

What was blossoming in the background? Technological advances were accelerating, enabling the financial industry to operate on a 24-hour basis around the globe. Companies were actively diversifying on the concept that 2 + 2 equaled 5. Brokerage firms became multi-product purveyors of financial products formerly distributed by banks and insurance companies. We witnessed a proliferation of product: options, tax shelters, oil and gas partnerships, cash management, equipment leasing, unit trusts, and zero-coupon bonds.

Meanwhile, a few astute observers in the industry began developing a better way to manage investments. Much was prompted by the Pension Reform Act of 1974 (ERISA) that encouraged active management of pension and profit sharing funds. Boutique investment firms were established to attract buy-and-hold assets managed by banks. Defined benefit plans were replaced by defined contribution plans.

James Lockwood, a successful registered representative at Dempsey-Tegeler in St. Louis, Missouri in the late 1960's recognized this sea change and became the intermediary between active, well-regarded investment managers and major institutional clients. This proved to be the segue that gave birth to separate account management for high net worth individuals. As initially conceived, it converted an equity salesperson into a consultant. Merrill Lynch's desire to bring Wall Street to the individual investor was advanced by EF Hutton's drive to bring professional money management to the high net worth investor. Jim Lockwood joined EF Hutton to intentionally convert an industry-changing concept into a major investment product.

Environmentally, Hutton was the perfect organization to encourage the development of the separately managed account business. It was the first brokerage firm to commit itself to building a fee-based business that would ensure a healthy revenue foundation in any business atmosphere. It offered an entrepreneurial environment, dedicated to developing new financial products, aggressively committed to the ongoing training of all its sales personnel and had a very identifiable marketing image. The newly formed money management area was welcomed by all facets of the organization and was given great latitude in developing the consulting area.

Additionally, Jim Lockwood had a great rapport with Bob Fomon the Chairman of EF Hutton and was given great autonomy. As an example, when Jim wanted to build an internal trust company, facilitating the consulting product development, Bob flew to Wilmington, Delaware, met with the Governor to ensure his support, hired Irving Shapiro of Skadden Arps, the most well-known attorney in the state (and former DuPont CEO), and suggested Jim join the most influential luncheon club in Wilmington. Bob approved moving the entire consulting division to Delaware after securing space in a building under construction, all in less than five business days from the initial request and many months before Hutton would be given approval to operate a Trust Company.

The separate account evolution that has grown so steadily since the early 1970s is not — and will not be — over. While Jim Lockwood and other pioneers mentioned in this book provided the initial thrust, many others—who are growing in numbers daily and are striving to help investors determine how to best allocate funds—are nurturing it. It has become, in its many iterations, the most intellectual financial process for investors to allocate capital based on changing economic needs.

This book is about the pioneers who established the industry and about the challenge that is now being passed to those embracing the concept of professional management for current and future generations of investors. The investor of tomorrow should not be deprived of their net worth or their retirement funds by acting as a do-it-yourself professional.

— JOSEPH LaMOTTA   — PETER F. MURATORE
CHAIRMAN EMERITUS   CHAIRMAN
OPPENHEIMER CAPITAL   MONEY MANAGEMENT INSTITUTE

The biggest challenge I faced while researching and writing "Legacy" was locating all of the individuals who were instrumental in moving the separately managed accounts business forward. Many of the early pioneers were easy to find because most are still active in the industry. Some, however, have passed away but the wonderful stories of their careers were shared with me by their close friends and colleagues.

Another challenge was trying to fit literally hundreds of interviews into fewer than 200 pages. Regrettably, it was not possible to include all of the talented industry veterans, but their firsthand accounts greatly impacted my research and enhanced the pages of this book.

It took about a year to complete "Legacy." As we put the book to press I was elated, but also saddened in a way. Elated because our industry would now have the opportunity to fully capture this wonderful history, but saddened as one would feel after reading the last page of a "familiar stranger's" diary. I say this because almost everyone I interviewed knew the legendary pioneer, Jim Lockwood—except me. Jim retired in the mid-80s and passed away in 1994 before I had the chance to know this great man. I spoke to Jim's wife, Audrie, and she kindly sent pictures of him and letters and other memorabilia to me. Audrie told me she and Jim met after one of his seminar presentations and they fell in love at first sight. "He ran home and told his brother, Emil, that he just met the woman he was going to marry," said Audrie. It was a love story lasting almost 30 years.

Jim Lockwood's love affair with this business lasted just as long. He worked tirelessly for his clients, with his partners and colleagues, and as a generous mentor to countless young and promising brokers and advisors. One of his protégés, Len Reinhart, even named his firm after him— a great testimony to Lockwood's influence.

Special thanks goes to Christopher Davis, Executive Director of the Money Management Institute for his encouragement, direction, and patience with me over the past year. Audrie Lockwood, Dennis Bertrum, Peter Muratore, John Ellis, Joe LaMotta, Tom Gorman, Dick Schilffarth and Len Reinhart deserve special recognition for the hours they spent walking down memory lane with me. Heartfelt appreciation to industry pioneer Dan Bott for introducing me to the world of fee-based business, and for giving me the opportunity to work with him during the formative years of IIMC.

Thanks also to my associate, Lyn Fisher, for her help with the interviews and for the meticulous production of this book, Lisa Gray, fellow writer, for her help with interviewing and writing, colleague Allen Plummer for his help with the chapter on education, Jim Marren for editing, and Christopher Gall for his beautiful cover illustration.

Finally, thank-you to the hundreds of advisors and consultants I was not able to interview, but who are, nonetheless, recognized and respected as dedicated and hard-working professionals who continue to carry on Jim Lockwood's legacy.

It truly was an honor being a part of bringing this book to life. I hope you enjoy reading it as much as I enjoyed writing it for you.

— Sydney LeBlanc, November 2002

"The ability to earn a premium income by rendering advice through a commission revenue stream was not something to bet your long-term livelihood on."

— James Lockwood

legendary consulting pioneer, 1965

1 | THE GENESIS OF SEPARATELY MANAGED ACCOUNTS

Many industry historians contend that the genesis of investment management consulting and separately managed accounts occurred on Wall Street in the early 60s. Others maintain that its origin was far from the stock exchanges, Fortune 500 companies, and pin-striped suits. What is the real legacy of separately managed accounts? Who are the pioneers who passed down the concept?

Throughout the pages of this book is the previously untold story of the emergence of an industry that had its roots in the institutional marketplace. It is the story of a profession in its infancy that was molded and sculpted by a handful of highly skilled visionaries and that, 30 years later, is embraced as a sophisticated, investment process-driven, client-centered service.

The concept of consulting, managed accounts and the investment process actually began in St. Louis, Michigan, a small town of 4,027 in the center of Michigan's lower peninsula, where, in the late 60s, a dedicated financial professional carved out a niche, then set out on a long and legendary journey to fill it. It's a rare consultant in the financial services industry who hasn't at least heard of his name, or the colorful stories about him.

This extraordinary man graduated from the U.S. Naval Academy at Annapolis in 1940 and was recognized as a war hero for his duty as a pilot on the carrier, Saratoga. After it was torpedoed the third time, he entered Naval flight training. In addition to being 'every man's general,' he also was an aristocrat of the highest order. His name was James Lockwood.

He also was the man prized as the most successful mutual fund salesman at Los Angeles-based Dempsey-Tegeler in the 60s, and who later became (to some) the innovative thorn in Dean Witter's side in the early 70s. Lockwood was the man ultimately responsible for spearheading and accelerating the concept of value through advice and the investment process for individuals, corporations and municipalities that previously were ignored.

But before we begin with tales about the men and women instrumental in educating and promoting investment management consulting and the managed account industry, let's properly set the stage and enjoy some history about the securities industry.

The Roots are Deep

The 60s and 70s were a time of significant political, social and economic change. As a result of several landmark pieces of legislation affecting pension funds, Wall Street witnessed remarkable changes in its markets and its players that would forever alter the way the financial services industry served institutional and retail investors.

Some of the most important new laws included:

- The Welfare and Pension Plan Disclosure Act Amendments of 1962, which shifted responsibility for protection of plan assets from participants to the federal government to prevent fraud and poor administration. These amendments came on the heels of the original Welfare and Pension Plan Disclosure Act of 1958 that established disclosure requirements to limit fiduciary abuse.

- The Self-Employed Individual Retirement Act of 1962, also known as the Keogh Act, made qualified pension plans available to self-employed persons, unincorporated small businesses, farmers, professionals, and their employees.

- The Tax Reform Act of 1969, which provided fundamental guidelines for the establishment and operation of pension plans administered jointly by an employer and a union.

- And, perhaps, the most significant of them all, ERISA, the Employee Retirement Income Security Act of 1974, which helped pave the way for early consulting visionaries to educate—and ultimately capture—the corporate and state defined benefit pension markets.

ERISA, of course, was designed to secure the benefits of participants in private pension plans through participation, vesting, funding, reporting, and disclosure rules. It established the Pension Benefit Guaranty Corporation (PBGC), and provided added pension incentives for the self-employed (through changes in Keogh plans) and for persons not covered by pensions (through individual retirement accounts, or IRAs). It established the legal status of employee stock ownership plans (ESOPs) as an employee benefit and codified stock bonus plans under the Internal Revenue Code.

It also established requirements for plan implementation and operation, the aspect of ERISA that ultimately allowed consultants to shine. ERISA mandated that plan assets be managed "prudently" (i.e., the Prudent Man Rule); otherwise, the corporation and the trustees would be held liable. The decision—or investment—process was required to be well-documented and followed, and someone always had to be accountable. As a result, many plan sponsors—municipal and corporate—chose to have investment professionals manage their assets. But many were ill-equipped to find the appropriate managers with which to align themselves.

Up until this time, most corporate and public funds, foundations and endowments, and estates were being managed by the large insurance companies and bank trust departments. Many assets were invested in balanced mutual funds. Prior to ERISA, some state-owned and corporate pension funds would buy their own stock, real estate, and bank CDs and would spend the pension money as their own. There was no true accountability.

Performance measurement was virtually unheard of and there were no benchmarks or similar vehicles to compare investment results. Banks and insurance companies held all of the cards and the plan sponsor's broker handled the transactions at the NYSE using fixed commission rates listed in the back of the Standard and Poor's guides.

INSTITUTIONAL CONSULTANTS EMERGE

In 1965, Harvard professor Michael C. Jensen conducted the first major study on the performance of mutual funds, and in 1968 AG Becker Corp. conducted the first major study of institutional plans. It was at that point that AG Becker gave rise to institutional consulting with their creation of the "Green Book" performance tables that compared performance results to benchmarks.

Armed with their research, AG Becker approached defined benefit plan sponsors urging them to measure the performance of the banks managing their pension funds. At the same time, they suggested that they would be pleased to provide performance measurement and portfolio monitoring services for the plan sponsors, thereby having numerous opportunities to obtain large institutional accounts whose trustees preferred not to involve themselves with the technicalities of quarterly performance comparison charts.

Around the same time, such firms as The Russell Company (Frank Russell) in Tacoma, Washington, and DeMarche Associates of Kansas City, SEI (part of AG Becker), and were busy gathering their own data on the performance of mutual funds. Armed with tangible information, they approached plan sponsors, offering help in researching, evaluating and selecting new managers for their funds. They presented multiple manager selection, asset allocation, investment policy statement guidance and other important steps in the investment process as mandated by ERISA. If all parties agreed, the consulting firms would receive the directed brokerage commissions in exchange for their recommendations, receiving soft dollars and, in time, valued referral business.

Said Craig Wainscott, Director, Knowledge Capital, Russell Investment Company, "The Russell Company was founded in 1936 and we were already providing a 'McKinsey' type of research for the pension funds. George Russell, the founder, was a talented and visionary man, who wanted to offer institutional consulting and high level asset allocation guidance to the top pension plans—well before most other firms were offering classic consulting services. We were doing manager evaluation and selection. Soon after we began providing performance measurement, and offered a competitive service to that of Becker." Wainscott said that JC Penney was so impressed by George Russell's presentation and quality of services, they became their first client, and remain so to this day.

In 1968, Edwin Callan, a major player in the institutional consulting business, formed the investment measurement division of Mitchum, Jones & Templeton. That firm was acquired by Paine Webber in 1973 and, soon after, Callan and some of his colleagues became fully independent by purchasing the performance division and forming Callan Associates, currently a leading investment management consulting authority.

Niche consulting firms, like Cambridge Associates, which was invited by Harvard University in the early 70s to conduct a comprehensive study of endowment management practices, discovered captive and lucrative audiences such as non-profit organizations. Butcher and Singer was also one of the first financial services firms to offer consulting services through their autonomous Butcher Consulting Group.

Many industry observers consider most of this activity to be the beginning of institutional consulting and the key individuals involved were among the first institutional investment management consultants.

THE LANDSCAPE CHANGES

Next, a series of events occurred in the financial services industry that further accelerated the trend toward skilled financial advisors capturing larger assets—the middle market, $50 - 150 million accounts, an under-serviced market that could truly benefit from the type of management that—until then—only Fortune 500 companies enjoyed.

The industry witnessed dramatic changes as talented portfolio managers at banks (looking closely at performance results and comparing them with the benchmarks) realized they could deliver superior investment performance for corporate clients, and departed to form their own independent firms.

A handful of leading brokers and advisors saw this evolution as their chance to differentiate themselves in the marketplace, add value, and provide counsel to small to mid-sized institutions. Working together as strategic partners, consultants and money managers now found it feasible to sit on the same side of the table with the client, using the investment process to guide them. An added benefit: Even though the trades were directed through the broker's firm, the inherent conflict of interest was eliminated by allowing the manager—instead of the broker— to make buy and sell decisions.

But there were dark days ahead. The Watergate scandal, President Nixon's eventual resignation, the Arab oil embargo and an economic recession forced our nation into the worst bear market since the 1930s. The Dow Jones Industrial Average's slide in 1973 was extremely volatile with severe losing streaks followed by sharp rallies. The Dow's close of 577 in December 1974 (45% off of its peak) was its lowest level since October 1962. More than ever, institutional and large investors needed sound advice and counsel to protect their assets.

Institutional trading continued to dominate the market, and since institutions were king, they demanded better rates. On May 1, 1975, "May Day" the Big Board's fixed commission rates were abolished and brokerage commissions became negotiable, giving rise to negotiated brokerage rates and—eventually—the discount brokerage phenomenon.

When this occurred, Jim Lockwood was quoted as saying, "As always is the case in an efficient capitalist system, once rates are no longer protected by a 'cartel' [NYSE], the rates don't go up, they go down. And over time, that revenue stream becomes less and less reliable because competition will ultimately drive it to the lowest cost service provider. So the ability to earn a premium income by rendering advice through commission revenue stream was not something to bet your long-term livelihood on."

Lockwood had that insight 30 years ago.

The New York Stock Exchange eventually was forced to do the right thing. The SEC handed down the directive. And a new era of competition began on Wall Street.

Sources: Pension Benefit Guarantee Corporation, Yanni-Bilkey, Journal of Finance

*"We knew the managed account business would be quite successful, but did I know it would grow into hundreds of millions of dollars? Well, of **course** not."*

— George Ball
former president of EF Hutton

While there are countless heroes in the managed account business, only a handful of pioneers are considered truly legendary. Visionaries Jim Lockwood, Joe LaMotta, John Ellis, Tom Gorman, and Dick Schilffarth are heralded to be among the original consulting and investment management scholars. We will visit with others who also are renowned for their quest for investment performance excellence for their clients. We'll also explore the question posed in Chapter One regarding whether consulting was conceived on Wall Street or on Main Street.

Meanwhile, in the early to mid–70s, astute observers of this new era on Wall Street wasted no time in creating an innovative business model that would provide the opportunity to capture lucrative, larger markets. Plus, it would immediately catapult them onto a more prestigious and professional level of client contact.

After the market debacle in '73-'74, small to mid–sized institutions, as well as affluent individuals, scurried for professional advice and counsel. Municipalities needed help investing their retirement fund assets since they had little experience participating in anything other than the bond markets. Who would tend to these markets?

HOW IT ALL BEGAN

Jim Lockwood, one of the first independent advisors in the financial services industry, began his industry career immediately after attending law school at the University of Pennsylvania. He joined the brokerage firm of Straus, Blosser & McDowell in the mid-50s. The Chicago-based firm had offices in Detroit, Grand Rapids, and Mount Clemens, Michigan. It was at this firm that he met John Ellis, a sales manager in the Chicago office. In 1963, Straus, Blosser & McDowell merged with Dempsey-Tegeler, a St.Louis-based firm, and both Jim and John were asked to serve on its board of directors.

Ellis said, "Jim became the largest producer at Dempsey and sold substantial amounts of mutual funds to corporations and wealthy individuals, specializing in Investment Company of America. In the early 60s, the firm was one of the very few selling mutual funds—not even Merrill Lynch would sign contracts with outside mutual funds."

In the late 60s, Capital Guardian Trust was formed by Ned Bailey (now deceased) and Robert Kirby, former principals of the Investment Company of America (still one of the great all-time mutual fund performers). Continued Ellis, "I hired Tom Gorman and he would make appointments to see pension fund treasurers, and Jim and I would tell the Capital Guardian story. In time, we consulted to the pension assets of such companies as John Deere, Household Finance, International Harvester, Field Enterprises, AO Smith and Abbott Labs. We also presented to these companies such managers as Supervised Investors of Chicago (which later became Kemper) with Carl Zerfoss, and Joe LaMotta of S&P InterCapital, who worked as an integral part of our team."

When Dempsey closed in 1970, the Lockwood team began looking for a new "home." Lockwood, Gorman, and Ellis found one at Dean Witter, where they continued prospecting large pension accounts. Also, not widely known is the fact that Lockwood's wife, Audrie—who was among a small number of female registered brokers at that time—handled Jim's retail business, allowing him to spend more time on the institutional side, and she did so until he retired.

Gorman, whose background included a successful advertising career in the radio business and ownership of an ad agency, recalled the early days. "After Dempsey-Tegeler was told by the NYSE in June, 1970 that it had a continuing capital deficiency and must be liquidated or sold, the three of us joined forces at Dean Witter," said Gorman.

In addition to Cap Guardian and S&P InterCapital (whose managed assets were subsequently acquired by Oppenheimer & Co., Inc.), Gorman said the trio worked with wise money managers such as Provident, Fiduciary Trust, and Bernstein McCauley. Tom Gorman is currently a retired consultant and executive director of Salomon Smith Barney's Association of Professional Investment Consultants (APIC) organization, a prestigious group of senior level consultants that grew from the original Alchemists Club. (See Chapter 3 for more information on the Alchemists.)

As the highest paid investment advisor at Dean Witter in the early 70s, Lockwood realized early on that municipalities could meet their actuarial return assumptions more effectively if they could step outside the heretofore "bond market only" investment restrictions and place some of their assets in the stock market.

Lockwood urged his brother, Emil, who held a Michigan State Senate seat around that time, to sponsor a bill recommending changes in the charters for city, county and state pension funds to allow up to 25% of the assets to be invested in the stock market. The bill gained favor and passed in 1968.

Dennis Bertrum, chairman and founder, Bank Street Advisors, who was a producing broker at the time for the regional firm First of Michigan and who would ultimately become national product manager for the consulting team at Hutton Investment Management, recalled this story: "As soon as the bill passed, Jim jumped in his private plane and visited the retirement fund investment committees for various municipalities in Michigan. He would introduce himself as an investment consultant, offering help in deciding who would manage their 25%."

After opening numerous accounts in his own state, he began prospecting municipalities in other states—as each of their legislatures enacted laws similar to the one adopted in Michigan. Lockwood already claimed strong relationships with venerable firms like Capital Guardian Trust and S&P InterCapital, headed by the highly skilled Joe LaMotta. Managers like these unhesitatingly joined the movement as they came to understand and believe in Lockwood's vision.

Said Bertrum of Jim Lockwood, "He worked with Capital Guardian and S&P and a few other managers who were willing to work on a 'directed' basis. For example, if a broker introduced a client to a money manager and the client hired that manager, the advisor would agree to run the portfolio transactions through the sponsoring brokerage firm. Back in those days [before "May Day"], commissions were fixed up to $500,000, so wherever the trades were directed, the client's costs were the same. All of the transacted business that ran through the firm accrued to the credit of the 'consulting' broker at absolutely no disadvantage to the client. At that time, fees as they are known today were not allowed. Lockwood did a lot of business in those early years introducing investment advisors to municipalities around the state."

Said Ellis about the fees, "No one was doing fees back then. However, a broker could get an exemption from the NYSE to manage a client's money for a flat fee, but in the 60s there were less than a dozen in the entire country who got the exemption. I recall the first broker to actually get an exemption and manage money for a client for a fee in lieu of a commission was the executive vice president for Dempsey on the West Coast. His name was Lou Whitney. He said he thought charging a commission was a conflict of interest."

A MEETING OF THE MINDS—DISAPPOINTMENT, THEN VICTORY

Dean Witter went public in 1971 and it was around that time LaMotta visited Lockwood with a revolutionary idea. Said LaMotta, "At the time, there was a tremendous amount of non-discretionary advisory accounts being handled for a very low fee— about

$700. The hand-holding and the personnel required to market to—and manage—that business was extraordinarily high. I also noticed in the Dean Witter prospectus that Jim Lockwood made in excess of one million dollars in 1969-70. I thought, 'This guy is earning more than the chairman of Dean Witter; I gotta meet this guy.' So I called him and set up a meeting. Basically, I said to him, 'You are a great marketer, and I think we at S&P are great investment managers. Why don't we do something together? I will convert our advisory accounts to discretionary management, and I'll talk with the clients about using Dean Witter as the executing broker, and in the meantime you continue getting accounts and recommending them to S&P InterCapital.' He said it was a great idea, and let's do it. It was as simple as that. I saw the spark in his eyes when I suggested the concept and, later, his commitment to it. He executed it marvelously."

About the same time, Dick Schilffarth was just beginning his new stint as a rookie broker in Milwaukee, Wisconsin with Dean Witter after selling his own highly successful business forms company. Schilffarth noticed, too, in the Dean Witter prospectus that Lockwood was an innovator and very highly paid for his efforts and soon arranged to meet with him and discuss Lockwood's ideas of being paid a fee in lieu of commissions, since this concept also appealed to Schilffarth. A synergy between the two soon developed.

In March 1973, Lockwood realized the scope and impact his concept would have on the investing public and on the industry. Knowing Dean Witter had the resources and the broker network to pioneer the way, Lockwood, Schilffarth, Gorman and Ellis put their heads together and developed a product that could be "sold" through the Dean Witter system, branding the firm as a consulting leader in the industry, all the while keeping money manager LaMotta in the loop.

Said Schilffarth, "We had a meeting and presented the concept of marketing our consulting program to brokers. My suggestion was to design it for small account programs, like the profit-sharing plan I had for my old manufacturing company. Out of that meeting sprang Dean Witter Plus [which later became EF Hutton Suggests]. The program had two managers: Boston Company Advisors and S&P InterCapital."

Initially, the "product" included the three-step process of drafting investment objectives, selecting and introducing suitable managers, and monitoring their ongoing performance.

Next, Lockwood and Ellis decided to approach the Dean Witter board and present the Dean Witter Plus product for their consideration. Gil Schubert, regional manager, arranged for their presentation to be an agenda item at the next board meeting. They flew to San Francisco, checked into the Fairmont Hotel and made the Dean Witter Plus presentation the next morning to their board. According to Ellis, "By the middle of the afternoon we hadn't heard a word so we called the executive offices, only to have the board secretary tell us the meeting had concluded and our Dean Witter Plus product was turned down. Ultimately, Bill Witter himself advised us that, 'The company did not want to raise money for outside managers.'"

When asked if the fact that Lockwood made more money than Bill Witter had anything to do with the rejection, Ellis said wryly, " Maybe Lockwood upstaged Bill Witter. Gil Schubert mentioned to me that Bill was not too happy that a 'salesman' in the Midwest made more money than he did. I'm sure it probably played in the decision somewhere, but after 30 years those details have all but faded." According to industry insiders, the real story is yet to be told.

Disappointed, but not ready to give up, the two went to dinner that evening to regroup. Bertrum recounted that one of Lockwood's favorite things in life was to have lavish dinners with fine wines and champagnes, all the while telling stories of his World War II years and his other adventures. Said Bertrum, "Jim was a raconteur of the highest degree and a great wine expert. Plus, he could hold forth on aspects of English literature and ancient history or mythology, physics—any subject you could name." Said Ellis, "He could recite poetry for hours on end. He was, without a doubt, the most brilliant man I ever knew."

Throughout the evening, Lockwood and Ellis brainstormed

on who could be their next viable partner.

EF Hutton Seizes an Opportunity

Armed with a revolutionary new program, but nowhere to go, Lockwood then called Ned Bailey, president of Capital Guardian Trust and asked for a brokerage firm referral. "Ned said that the up-and-coming firm on the Street was E.F. Hutton," recalled Schilffarth, "and so Jim called George Ball, president at Hutton."

On Sunday morning, April 8, 1973, Ball held a meeting in the New York office that included himself, chairman Bob Fomon, chief operating officer Norman Epstein (creator of the BPS system. See Chapter 8) Lockwood and Ellis. George Ball, now chairman of the board at investment banking firm Sanders, Morris, Harris, said, "I was very aware of the psychological conflict of commissions and performance. When I was a broker I tended to trade too little for clients, and I used to think it was shame we couldn't charge clients on a fee basis. When Jim and John came to me I felt the concept was a low-cost, low-risk way to try something that, intellectually, I had been espousing to others because I really believed in the concept."

Ball said that, at the time, managers were "hungry for money to manage" and by giving up the administrative functions and the costs, it would be a highly profitable business for them, as they would capture assets they wouldn't have otherwise.

Peter Muratore, currently chairman of the Money Management Institute's Board of Governors and, at that time, the national manager of marketing at Hutton, met Lockwood and Ellis during that meeting. "I thought it was a very intriguing project, and that it would be a very significant concept for the brokers who wanted out of the transaction business," said Muratore. "George asked me to take Jim under my wing, and we worked together from 1973 until 1987. At the time we joined forces, Hutton had 3,500 reps and that number doubled over the following decade."

Said Ball, "We all agreed it would take a while for the fee concept to be embraced, but that its growth would probably wind up being logarithmic, not arithmetic. And we knew it would be quite successful, but did I know it would grow into hundreds of millions of dollars? Well, of course not."

Muratore added, "Hutton made the decision that we were going to attempt to cover our fixed costs with our fee revenues. That's why Hutton was so aggressive in developing new products, especially financial products that were fee-based. This concept really started before Jim Lockwood came aboard—we were already in the insurance and annuity business. Jim's concept fit in perfectly with where we wanted to take the firm."

Elated with the receptive tone of the meetings, Lockwood waited for a contract from Hutton. It arrived within days and on April 18, 1973 he and Ellis announced they were leaving Dean Witter and were going to Hutton to form a new department they referred to as "The Consulting Group." After firing off an internal memo to the executive committee about the loss of the team, regional manager and Lockwood's biggest supporter, Gil Schubert, resigned shortly thereafter.

Some sources say—and it's arguable— that Ball was less concerned about the Dean Witter Plus program than he was about capturing more than $1 million in gross commissions from Lockwood and Ellis. John Daly, Vice President and Senior Marketing Representative for Jennison Capital, had this to say: "Hutton knew it was the right thing to do for clients. It was very difficult for them in the beginning; they were starting from scratch with a new concept. The biggest hurdle that they had to get over was convincing brokers it was the best thing they have ever done – not only for their clients but also for themselves in terms of building business."

Said Ball, "Jim and John had excellent business when they came over, and I guess you could say, in a sense, that played some role in the decision. But, these men were individuals of substance and honor and that was very important to me. Jim Lockwood was enormously charismatic and John Ellis was enormously plausible, and they sold themselves to me. But, I did have a strong bias. I heard an idea I had been espousing for years, and I was inclined to agree with their concept."

After brief negotiations, Lockwood engineered a unique contract for himself. It allowed him to live in New York Monday through Thursday and fly to his new home in Florida for a three-day weekend in the winter, and to his home in Michigan in the summer. Said Bertrum, "I remember he would arrive at lunchtime on Monday and by 1 p.m. his desk was clear and it stayed clear until he left on Thursday. There was nothing on top of his desk, ever. He was the most organized man I ever met."

The Consulting Group Accelerates

Dean Witter had no idea at the time what was walking out the door. Perhaps one of the reasons why they might not have been keen on Lockwood's idea was that they already had a substantial asset management division, and also a very strong corporate finance department. Their corporate finance people were calling on the same institutions that Lockwood was, but were selling investments, not consulting.

Said Bertrum, "Even though he was 'selling' money managers, because of the heavy power base at the firm it was very easy to knock the Lockwood-types out of the way. The political environment within Hutton was 'clean.' The Consulting Group could get on without a lot of naysayers."

Hutton was, at the time, the most fertile ground for creative men and women in the industry. The firm was the great innovator of Wall Street. Out of Hutton came Suggests, wrap fees, private equity and direct investments, universal life insurance, and 12-b1 fees, among other innovations. "Fomon and Ball were the greatest team ever," said Schilffarth. "Together they were unstoppable. They thrived on the entrepreneurial spirit and drew that caliber of brokers."

Lockwood and Ellis set up a department whose basic mission was to find corporate and government clients, provide consulting services, and create a revenue stream. Originally, they began as a direct sales operation; in other words, initially they were not expected to train other brokers, just to generate revenues on their own.

Said Muratore, "It took about a year, but we linked up with three managers to run the money: Provident, Capital Guardian Trust (American Funds) and Joe LaMotta's S&P InterCapital. Joe was the most aggressive of the three managers and had outstanding performance. He put in a tremendous amount of time marketing his firm as a portfolio manager." Said Ball, "Yes it took about a year, but we realized we had a winner of a program. Dick Schilffarth was very evangelistic about spreading the message, and people listened." Schilffarth, in short order, respectfully gained the nickname of "preacher man" from some of his colleagues.

Joe LaMotta, now retired CEO and Chairman of Oppenheimer Capital (which acquired the S&P entities in 1975) said, "There were really only two boutique managers back then—S&P InterCapital and Jennison Associates. I was with Standard & Poor's Corp. when it spun off its advisory business into S&P InterCapital in 1968 and a group of seven highly talented individuals ran the new firm." LaMotta said that after S&P InterCapital was sold to Oppenheimer most of the group went on to become CEOs of major firms.

In late spring of 1973, EF Hutton opened a new office in Milwaukee for Dick Schilffarth and recruitment for new brokers began. Later that year EF Hutton Suggests was ready to go into the field with three managers. Said Schilffarth, " I met a young man in the Denver office of Hutton whose name was John Vann— he had just been licensed in August. He had a prospect he wanted us to call on, and her name was Hilda Peck. She was 75 years old and had $49,000 to invest. Because of the low minimum, The Boston Company took it instead of S&P. And that was the first separately managed account that we had an individual broker open."

Daniel R. Bott, Sr., CIMC, Managing Director, Bott & Associates, Investment Consulting Group of First Union Securities in Arizona, an industry pioneer and former chairman emeritus of the Institute for Certified Investment Management Consultants (now IMCA), had this to say about Hutton's eagerness to embrace the consulting process: "It was looked upon as a form of institutional work, but with a different approach. Institutional sales basically involved calling on money managers to sell them investments. The Consulting Group called on clients and introduced them to money managers. It was a roundabout– a totally new and different perspective. Hutton accepted the concept. Their philosophy was if the firm wasn't successful in getting *all* of the business using their own internal managers [running retirement plans or high net worth accounts], then maybe they could get *half* of the business by being the broker-consultant who placed the money manager with them. It was an open environment. They had a great culture and a management team that supported entrepreneurship and new ideas. Other firms were saying, if they couldn't control all of the revenue, they didn't want any of it; they were very short-sighted."

Said Bob Leo, Vice Chairman, MFS Investment Management, "In the late 70s and early 80s, every broker in my office at Shearson in Dayton was doing some form of their own managed money. Managed commodity funds were big, and is a very important piece of the history of this business. A lot of brokers got their start working with managers through the commodity business, and it was quite successful." As their biggest producer and manager in the 70s, Leo also worked for Shearson's predecessor Hayden Stone, all the while specializing in retail and institutional managed money. "I brought in Dean and Associates, Cincinnati Renaissance, and Mead Adam and Co. to manage the money, but we didn't even think about asking for fees, only the directed trades." Bob Leo relocated to New York City after being appointed Shearson's national sales manager in 1984.

"NEGOTIATE THE COMMISSIONS TO ZERO"

May Day may have been one of Lockwood's finest hours, because when fixed commissions were abolished, firms were panicked over how to protect their revenue stream. Lockwood's answer was to "let it go." He was quoted by a colleague as saying, "If commissions are negotiable, then let's negotiate them right down to zero." Lockwood presented himself as an investment consultant, not a broker. He firmly believed if he removed the commissions, he eliminated all conflicts of interest to the client. This was absolutely revolutionary at that time.

During a meeting with George Ball, Lockwood asked how much of a fee should they charge. After a few minutes of calculations, someone said, "How about 3%?" (which, at the time was less than the 5% return on assets of trading accounts). Without much discussion, everyone in the meeting agreed. Said Ball, "The 3% was totally pulled out of the air. There was a little back-of-the-envelope arithmetic, and after a few minutes I said, 'let's try 3%' and that was it."

It was at that time that Dick Schilffarth was credited for having coined the term "wrap fee." Said Schilffarth with a hint of wry humor, "Yes, I acknowledge it, I admit it, and I also apologize for it."

Today, it's generally accepted that the term wrap fee does not adequately reflect the true definition or comprehensiveness of separately managed accounts. Rather, it focuses on the fee aspect only, and not the significant value of the investment process and the consulting effort of the advisor. Increasingly, the industry is using such terms as separately managed accounts (SMAs), managed accounts, separate accounts, fee-based business and managed money interchangeably to describe this area of investment strategy. The focus is on the process, and not the actual product or fee.

In October 1975, the first product to be offered to the public on an all-inclusive fee basis was labeled Hutton Investment Management (HIM). Six months from May Day Hutton rolled out a product that discounted commissions to zero. Said Bertrum, "It was way ahead of its time since the wrap fee phenomenon really didn't occur until Hutton Select Managers in 1987."

Schilffarth related a story about the first ad that ran announcing HIM seminars. "In May 1976 I wrote a training manual and did our first training session. We presented Hutton Investment Management to the 15 best branches we had in late November 1976. We created and paid for the ads if they would do the seminars. The Boulder branch office ran our 'Have You Heard About HIM' ad in the local newspaper. Sometime before the seminars, the branch manager said the ad wasn't that effective because they only got three responses: one from a Merrill broker wanting to figure out what we were doing, and the other two callers wanted to know what time the revival meeting started."

BACHE AND HUTTON: PARALLEL WORLDS

While Lockwood and the Group were busy gathering assets, recruiting, and training brokers, Vic Rosasco, CIMA, Sr Vice President, Prudential Securities was doing institutional consulting at Bache Halsey Stuart Shields. Rosasco, a consulting pioneer who entered the securities industry in 1955, joined Bache's Asset Management Services Group in 1976, and started his own investment management consulting career.

Rosasco and colleague Richard "Richie" Klitzberg (who began working with money managers in 1972 under the direction of industry pioneer Jim Owen, co-founder of the Investment Management Consultants Association) worked together providing institutional consulting services. Rosasco, later promoted to west coast regional coordinator for the Group at Bache, said they had eight members, including pioneer Hal Rossen, now a senior consultant at Morgan Stanley. Each member had a region and considerable due diligence responsibility. They followed up on the brokers' leads and helped them open the consulting accounts.

According to Rosasco, the differences in consulting models between Hutton and Bache were that Bache wanted to control the quality of the services. They didn't want 600-plus brokers selling consulting services if they were not expert at it. Their target was the larger institutional business, and that's what they went after, while Hutton went after small-to mid-sized markets. Even though Bache started around the same time Hutton did [with Jim Lockwood] they never came close to the stage of Hutton's revenue. Bache only wanted to look at accounts of $25 million and up.

Jim Owen, who is credited with launching the consulting services business at Bache, was a broker in their Lexington, Kentucky office. Owen ultimately moved to New York to run the firm's Asset Management Services Group, but left in 1976 to join Stephenson and Company, then eventually on to NWQ Investment Management in the 80s. Bache was acquired by Prudential Insurance in 1981 and changed its name the following year to Prudential-Bache.

Technology in the "Dark Ages"

As the HIM program was gathering momentum, so was the administrative aspect Schilffarth hired a young woman named Judy Rice, currently President, Prudential Investments, to run the administration for HIM. "It was truly an interesting time because all of the business was done manually," said Rice. "I got the infrastructure up and running, and worked with the portfolio managers. I was the only one doing the work, and literally, had to take the status sheets [for the trades] home with me and continue working. The biggest thing was I had to code tickets for 'no commissions' if we were making trades in the account for money managers and I had to do that, ticket by ticket, trade by trade. Block orders were done manually too, and there was no automatic way to track client restrictions, so I had to keep a spreadsheet of what the restrictions were, like no tobacco or liquor stocks in the account."

Rice said that with no fax machines and no emails, the process was time-intensive; in addition, every time a trade was completed for a client, a personal letter was sent explaining the purchases in the account. "We were very client-service oriented, but it took an enormous amount of time to do all this paperwork. One day, I just picked up the phone and called George Ball and introduced myself and told him I was having problems with the 'no commission'" paperwork, and I needed help from the programmers—now. He said, 'I will get it done, Judy.' It was like that at Hutton."

Hutton Investment Management was a portfolio management service provided by a staff of portfolio managers under the direction of Allen Goldberg, who was director of research at Hutton. He was given the product and managed the portfolios on a 3% fee. The minimum account size was $25,000, and the average HIM holdings in a portfolio were less than 20 stocks. Soon after, new research director Alan J. Miller took the reins and is credited with making a significant impact on HIM and building it to its highest level. "He ran the first wrap fee product ever," said Bertrum of Miller.

Muratore recounted a story about Miller in the early days. "When we decided to do internal management, Alan said he wanted to be the portfolio manager. When we asked him what his style was, he said 'eclectic.' After Alan established a portfolio, I started getting complaints that there was no movement in the portfolios. I said, 'Alan, you have to make some trades, even if they are cosmetic, because our clients don't feel they should pay a 3% fee annually when there are no trades, and they are not convinced anyone is watching their portfolios.' He said he liked the portfolios the way they were and he wasn't going to make any trades. About three months later, we continued getting complaints so, once again, I pressured him to make some trades. Finally, I asked George Ball to talk to him. George tried to influence him into making a least one trade per year. We went round and round with Alan. Come to think of it, I don't think he ever made a trade!"

Muratore eventually had 20 product managers reporting to him. Annually they would present their separate business plans. He said he always looked forward to seeing Jim's plan because it was never the same as the previous year's. Said Muratore, "He always had new ideas for product or training programs, new packaging, new fee structures. It was such a pleasure to experience his innovative spirit. Not only was he interested in separate accounts, but he always showed great enthusiasm for marketing and business development. As a result, there was constant 'renewed' energy that ran through the department."

Recalled William Turchyn, partner, Mariner Investment Group, a premier hedge fund manager, and co-chair of the Money Management Institute's Executive Committee of the Board of Governors, "Lockwood was quite a character. When I was at Hutton in the 70s, we used to talk about each other's businesses, and he used to kid me saying, 'why do you re-invent your business every year? I don't need to do that because I am building an asset management business.' Well, he really influenced my thinking about how we built investment solutions. He talked about the consulting process, asset allocation, the long-term approach to successful investing. We used to have fascinating discussions about not limiting our thinking to the kinds of investments that could fit within an asset allocation—like paintings and collectibles. We actually talked about investing in a fund of works of art. We decided not to, but it was those types of creative sessions that led to innovation, and the eventual success of managed accounts."

"When we began training brokers in the system, we were looked upon as lepers. They said,'You want me to do WHAT for three percent?'"

— Frank Campanale, CEO
Salomon Smith Barney Consulting Group

The allure of managed accounts and investment management consulting continued to spread, albeit slowly, throughout the industry, and brokers who appreciated the investment process embraced the concept. According to industry sources there were approximately 100 consulting brokers and advisors by the mid-70s, but the number kept climbing.

Interestingly, whenever the industry faced a crisis—such as when tax shelters dried up, by 1987—the consultants were the ones who surfaced unscathed. Consequently, big producers like those doing the shelter business looked to consulting and managed accounts as the new rewarding —and value-added— area in which to be involved. After all, they were already comfortable with wealthy clients and simply needed a new way to serve their needs.

Their firms, skeptical but curious, began testing the waters to learn if there really were opportunities in this niche. But obstacles soon began to get in the way of doing business. It became a political minefield within the ranks.

Internal Conflicts

Leonard A. Reinhart, currently chairman and CEO of Lockwood Financial Group in Malvern, Pa. (he named his firm after Jim Lockwood, his long-time friend and mentor), joined Jim Lockwood at Hutton in the spring of 1978. John Ellis was running the institutional side of the business and Dick Schillfarth was working with Suggests—and later, HIM— and training brokers. Said Reinhart, "When I joined, I found there was no formalized research in place for evaluating and choosing money managers. It was basically just in-person manager interviews. I was brought on as an analyst to evaluate the managers, because the competition on the institutional side was becoming more analytical in nature: performance measurement and monitoring. We needed to look closely at the technology of doing this business."

Even the traditional stockbrokers had a difficult time with how they reported to their own clients. Recalled Frank Campanale, currently CEO of Salomon Smith Barney Consulting Group (the heir to the Hutton program), "I remember at the beginning of my career at EF Hutton that, as stockbrokers, we weren't even allowed to show a client a P/L statement. We weren't allowed to develop one, so the client never knew at the end of the year whether they were making money or losing money – they had to figure it out with their accountants. I knew, even back then, something had to be done."

At Hutton, the consultants also needed a separate trading desk. Reinhart explained, "Reason was, if the block desk handled the business, they wanted commissions. Since we [consultants] were doing zero commissions, they weren't terribly interested in helping trade the business for the money managers. So, we had to create our own trading desk. As John Ellis would say to us, 'We're like a destroyer, but all of our guns are pointing at each other.' " It was finally agreed upon to give the consulting division its own trading desk as part of its eventual transfer to Delaware.

Peter Muratore recounted, "We were driving the institutional people crazy. We wanted to be first in this business, so Hutton spared no expense in the technology department. That's when

Lenny [Reinhart] came on board. We had a big jump on the rest of the industry and we wanted to maintain that lead."

Reinhart, a long-time colleague of Muratore's, said, "Since we were doing everything ourselves for the first time, no one was really that eager to help us. Jim set up a bonus pool—based on the profitability of the product—that compensated the people in consulting services." Muratore recounted the story of how he renegotiated Lockwood's contract every two or three years. "The bonus pool was important to Jim, as was financially compensating his people for their good work," he said, " and he never argued with me about having to either cut his compensation back or change it in some way. His business was growing so rapidly that he quickly made up for whatever we had to cut back. This re-negotiation went on for about 15 years because his compensation just kept going up. That's how successful he was."

Reinhart talked about the early operations, "We built our own operations department and our own quarterly reporting system. Invariably, two or three years down the road, new management would come in and ask why our product area had its own operations department. Then they'd move it to New York and it would get messed up, and we'd end up having to take it back. It was frustrating for us because we were trying to launch a new type of business in an old brokerage firm infrastructure. We were fortunate in that as long as we made money for the firm, there were no complaints." (See more on technology in Chapter 8.)

The same problem was pervasive at other brokerage firms as the consulting business began to grow. It was no secret that the institutional desks were placed on a pedestal. Their brokers were more sophisticated, more respected, and traditionally much bigger producers. There existed a "discrimination" of sorts against the retail brokers. "The perception was," said Dan Bott, "that the institutional brokers were entitled to the business, but not the retail brokers. ERISA was so new, there was a lack of appreciation for pension plan regulation that mandated the sponsors receive all of the value they could from their investment. In essence, the commission dollars didn't belong to the money manager; they really belonged to the client. That's when the battle began."

Continued Bott, "The larger retail brokers left and either joined SEI or set up such firms as Wilshire and Associates and Performance Analytics. I had the same conflicts when I was at Kidder Peabody in the early days. I would ask my pension plan clients to sign a letter specifying where they wanted their business to go."

Institutional brokers and retail brokers continued to jockey for their positions at their own firms until many others decided to look for more friendly "environments" in which to work. This battle of control waged on well into the early 80s. Kidder Peabody and Dean Witter chose not to encourage the business at the time, allowing Hutton to keep the consulting crown until both firms decided to take another look in 1986. Dean Witter took a different, more cautious, approach and launched the first wrap fee program with their own internal money managers.

Said Bott, "In order for Dean Witter to get around the institutional business conflict, they decided to support managed accounts at the low end—under $1 million for the brokers-at-large."

Other Wall Street firms fought allowing brokers to participate at the higher end, too. But another conflict occurred when it became clear that, as they recruited top producers, many of them had institutional accounts. The managed account engine couldn't be slowed. The firms were finally realizing the potential gain through the books of their large producers. Said Bott, "For example, in 1990, when Merrill bought out the Florida operation of Kidder Peabody where my brother Jerry worked, they captured about 15% of their business from Jerry alone. That was the beginning of the end of the period when large firms put the kibosh on producers going after big accounts."

Said Muratore, "We recruited large producers from other firms, and the separately managed account concept really excited them. It also helped us retain our large producers."

Hutton Becomes the Training Baron

As Dennis Bertrum is known to say, " If there is one word that distinguishes the intellectual history of consulting services, it is education." This was—and continues to be— one of the major gaps in the continuation and promotion of managed accounts in the securities industry. Education and training of brokers and advisors in the investment process, in due diligence and in the marketing and servicing of managed accounts to the wealthy as well as small to mid-sized institutions eluded many firms.

Said Bertrum, "Hutton succeeded in this area so incredibly well because the Consulting Group taught brokers to work more effectively with their clients. It was the Group's training, funded by Hutton, but the members of the group were left to do their own educating because they wanted to control the quality and accuracy of the message. So it never got out of our [the Group's] hands." Muratore was responsible for training at Hutton and he ensured that every training program included a consulting services module on all subjects for both sales and management. All new sales training programs contained large time allotments directed at all fee based financial products.

This was groundbreaking, especially during a time when the industry was all transaction-based, and preaching the fee-based message was virtually unheard of and often shunned. Recalled Campanale about brokers' reactions, "When we began training brokers in the system, we were looked upon as lepers. 'You want me to do WHAT for three percent?' they would say. Don't forget, the average return on assets in a trading account at that time was between five and six percent."

Campanale talked about obstacles and objections they had to overcome with clients too, but noted that, after a logical discussion of fees, most were convinced fees were the best option. He said, "One day, we were making a presentation for a client back in 1976, and we said, 'here are the four steps: We're going to write investment guidelines, make an asset allocation recommendation, conduct a manager search and hire the managers, then do the ongoing monitoring and evaluation'. The client said, 'That's a very logical, analytical approach, I like that. But, how do I know you're not in cahoots with the money manager and you aren't just going to churn my accounts for commissions because I'm giving you discretion?' We explained that we would charge one fee of 3% and all transactions would be included. It was simple as that, especially in light of what the client could have paid in commissions."

The majority of brokers, though, turned a deaf ear to managed accounts. Muratore, who was also in charge of marketing and national product management for Hutton, recalled giving at least three speeches a week to various brokers from visiting branches on how to build a managed account business. He traveled extensively teaching the concept. Today, his colleagues say he was light-years ahead of his time.

"I used to tell brokers that they needed to be on the same side of the desk as their clients," said Muratore. "At that time, Hutton had a Director's Advisory Council [DAC] that consisted of the 25 biggest producers in the firm, but eventually it slowly started leaning toward those brokers who were doing the consulting business instead of transactions. Unfortunately, a lot of them rejected the concept because many of them didn't understand the total concept, and that it wasn't just another way to do financial planning."

Said Bertrum of Hutton's success, "I believe the real reason Hutton was so eminently successful in the promotion of consulting services to our brokers is directly traceable to the Herculean efforts of one man: Dick Schillfarth. He had great zeal and was a highly effective educator. He used to wear the American flag on his lapel—and still does to this day. He would go out and tell the story. He was great organizer and promoter, was absolutely tireless, working long hours and doing lots of traveling."

Dick Schillfarth was as great at marketing the business as Jim Lockwood was at creating it. Said Bertrum, "Schillfarth realized that not only do you package the business and educate the brokers, but you must recognize them as well. Brokers need constant care and feeding. This is the recipe, and it was the marvelous mystique of Hutton. They were the best in recognizing their people. So with that in mind, Schillfarth created the Alchemists Club."

This group comprised those advisors who generated a significant amount of revenue providing consulting services to their clients. The first meeting of the five original members of the Alchemists Club was held in 1975. Said Reinhart, "The Senior Alchemists really got to know each other, became friends, went on trips together with their spouses, and soon a certain sub-culture grew from the Alchemists within this big brokerage firm. It was a tight knit group. Our group became known as the 'country club' since our advisors were not in the office all day and the others assumed they were out golfing."

The Club blossomed to include such consultants as Dick Oliver, Tom Clark, Tom Mulvaney, Larry Kykendall, Rick Miles, Bill Chambers, Don Torget, David and Brenda Blisk, and Les Griffin, among others. The Alchemists Club ultimately grew to where it is today—at around 600-plus members—but has since been re-named after the Shearson merger with Smith Barney. It is now known in the industry as the Association of Professional Investment Consultants (APIC) and is within the Salomon Smith Barney "college" for consultants, as some refer to it.

Said Bertrum, "The incredible thing is that today the core group of senior alchemists have either retired from SSB or are still there. Because they have built such an incredible annuity for themselves there was no reason to go to another firm."

Growth of the Programs

Shortly after October 1975 once the initial wrap fee was actually implemented and the billing systems were in place, Lockwood introduced EF Hutton Suggests Type One, Two, Three and Four. The popular programs were One and Three: Securities custodied at Hutton with no directed commission, all trading done commission free, and the client paid the fee. Said Bertrum, "The 3% became a negotiable point with institutions for certain minimum support very early on."

By 1979 the Hutton force had grown to about 6,000 reps, almost triple the number six years earlier, attracting entrepreneurial brokers—big producers and advisors who had heard about the power of the Consulting Group and who also wanted to do consulting and managed accounts. As part of this growth Hutton began opening branches in the suburbs and cities, and the entrepreneurial spirit inside Hutton continued to spread.

In April 1979, under the direction of Peter Hageman, Hutton Capital Management was created and in April 1980 Hutton Portfolio Management was launched. "This allowed our brokers to be fee-paid, fully discretionary money managers," said Schilffarth. "That was a great program. It took 160 very intense hours for the training and was well received."

Much later, on April 29, 1988, the shareholders at Shearson Lehman Bros approved the merger of Hutton. When Hutton was sold, the Consulting Group was the "crown jewel" in the package, said Campanale, "Hutton was widely recognized as having the best retail business in the industry."

*"I was doing every-
thing from managing
accounts to marketing
to stuffing brochures."*

— Muffet Arroll, Managing Partner, AMVESCAP

The growing interest for entry into the managed account business was not limited to the pioneering consultants, EF Hutton and their advisors. Enthusiasm was brewing outside of Hutton among other firms, other advisors, and, particularly, the newly independent money managers themselves. Said Peter Muratore, "We had [at Hutton] a continual stream of management visitors from other firms to see what we were doing."

The managed account concept changed the face of the entire industry, and the money managers who broke away from the banks and insurance companies to launch their own firms were poised to participate in one of the most significant shifts in the history of the industry.

To this group it truly was a new era.

"In the 80s," said Grace Fey, Executive Vice President and Director of Frontier Capital Management Company, "there were only one or two managed account programs. EF Hutton's was the first and it gave a new definition to the way brokers and money managers worked together." Oppenheimer Capital [S&P Intercapital] was the other, led by Joe LaMotta, which became and remained one of the major participants in the managed account business throughout Hutton's ultimate acquisition by Shearson Lehman Bros.

Advisory accounts at S&P InterCapital were difficult and laborious to manage. According to LaMotta, the desire to develop a more efficient business was the driving force that led him to Jim Lockwood to discuss the viability of managed accounts. "I can't take any credit for what happened after Jim ran with the idea to Hutton. But I take a great deal of pride in the fact that I was one of the early pioneers of the managed account business," said LaMotta.

Formation of the Early Managers

There are many stories about how these new money management firms entered the business as well as the many common threads running through them all. For example, they all had prior relationships that allowed them to more easily segue from their institutional and bank trust department focus to working with individual investors and their advisors. They all were innovative, forward-thinking individuals who recognized that the new way of doing business was good for themselves and their clients.

The managers began networking and sharing names of those advisors who were involved in the retail managed account business because they realized it was a significant way to leverage their business and gain more assets under management. Most firms were heavily involved in organizations like The Investment Management Consultants Association (IMCA) and, at that time, The Institute for Investment Management Consultants (IIMC), which were in their infancy in the mid-80s, and this further helped build the networks and spread the managed account concept.

The higher-level broker/consultant market was also a ripe one, and many managers played the dual role of educating not only their new clients, but the brokers and advisors as well.

Fresh Starts

"I promise you, at the time we started our firm in the mid-80s, you couldn't have filled 40 seats with retail brokers who where working with managers," reminisced Frank Gibb, President and co-founder of Godsey and Gibb Associates. " That was really an institutional area. We all shared names [of brokers to call] – it really was a fun time." Gibb and Joe Godsey, his partner at the time, believed in the new way of doing business and realized the market was wide open. The belief in the concept was so great they laid everything on the line and took the plunge together.

According to Gibb, the firm had no assets at the outset. Gibb's strength was in marketing so he began making presentations to brokers and their firms. They mailed quarterly newsletters and followed up with in-person meetings. "We'd go in to the presentation and sell the client on the concept of managed accounts," said Gibb. "We'd also sell it to the broker/consultant. That's why our firm received such tremendous acceptance initially. We would help brokers build their business and teach them about objectives, risk tolerances, and management style. We built a reputation for ourselves – 'if you want to get the business, use Godsey and Gibb and have Frank Gibb come in and make the presentation.'"

Said Janet Mariconti, Sr. Vice President, Prudential Financial, "When I entered the managed account business at Neuberger and we began our relationship in 1988 with the Merrill Lynch Consults program, it was very clear that clients were less familiar with the process of separately managed accounts. They were more accustomed to getting the product or stock du jour from their financial consultant. So few were accustomed to the consultative approach that the managed account industry was putting in place."

Another early entrant, Calamos Asset Management, Inc. was founded in 1977. Said John Calamos, Chairman, CEO, Chief Investment Officer and founder of the firm, "We were a specialty money management firm dealing in convertible security strategies, which was a very unique type of strategy at the time and still is." The firm primarily was dealing with institutional clients until the late 70s-early 80s, when they began developing relationships with brokers who understood their investment strategies."

He continued, "I developed very specific strategies I believed would work well in the marketplace, specifically, convertible strategies— and I thought the best way to exercise my professional abilities as a money manager would be through my own firm. It gave me the freedom and flexibility to create a unique strategy."

Back in those days, said Calamos, "Broker/consultants had much more of an open mind about unique strategies than the institutional consultants – they really didn't seem to have an open mind about anything!" Calamos, along with Invesco, was one of the original 16 managers recommended by the Hutton Consulting Group.

TRUST DEPARTMENT MIGRATION

Recalled Muffet Arroll—who is managing partner at the firm's holding company Amvescap, "Invesco was the investment counseling division of The Citizens and Southern National Bank, now Bank of America. It was a wholly owned subsidiary of the bank and in 1979, Charles Brady and eight other partners bought the business from the bank. John Ellis was the consultant on one of the largest accounts at the bank and he and the Invesco partners got to be friends over the years."

Ellis called Brady in the mid-80s to discuss the manager programs they were developing at Hutton. The concept of handing client servicing over to the broker/consultants and concentrating solely on managing the assets was very attractive. The appeal of entering a fresh market and having access to that market's assets was undeniable.

Said First Union's Dan Bott, "It was easier to convince higher-minimum managers to accept lower minimums because the order entry and account record-keeping systems were automated and the brokerage firm [Hutton] would provide that. The manager wasn't required to do any of the billing or have any client communication. They could focus on running the portfolio. The concept was sold to the manager as a way to get business they normally wouldn't get. Managers liked it, had a good relationship with the firm, and were in a good position to pick up some of the larger institutional accounts when they came along."

"It was Hutton's willingness to take on the higher mainte-nance aspects of the accounts that successfully wooed Invesco," added Arroll. "It was all about leverage." The only way Invesco and other early entrants in this market would have been able to work with low account minimums would have been to double their sales forces to meet with significant numbers of new clients on a regular basis.

About the same time, Grace Fey and three partners broke away from Massachusetts Investment Management Company and formed their own firm, Winchester Capital Management. "We were al-ready working with a couple of broker/consultants who were big producers," Fey said, "so we were looking for ways to lever-age the relationships we already had — where could we get the most clients for the least cost? Where would our marketing be most effective?"

The answer was obvious. The firm lowered minimums from $1 million to $250,000, in one fell swoop. Brokers and advisors at the time were making an effort to work with outside money man-agers, but the industry was very fragmented. "We determined when we started our firm that we would try the same route we used when we were part of Massachusetts Investment Management and it was very advantageous," Fey added. "We thought it was going to be great in terms of distribution."

CHALLENGES TO ENTRY: TIME FOR ORGANIZATION

The early entrants certainly had their challenges along with the excitement of gaining access to new markets and more assets. It was an interesting time because the process was new to everyone. But there were no substantial infrastructures, no large sales forces as we see today. "I was asked to head the program at Invesco," said Arroll, "and I was doing everything from managing accounts to marketing to stuffing brochures. It sounds like it was a lot, but the demands at that time were quite different than they are today. No one expected glossy materials or expected you to be out there all the time, so we grew up in it together, so to speak."

While many of the money managers were taking advantage of

the brokerage firms' technology, Calamos developed its own system. "We created our own software in-house," said John Calamos. "It was a wrap program, but it was mainly under separate investment management agreements." This meant the client would make one agreement with Hutton and a separate agreement with Calamos.

Hutton, at the time, was the only firm with an established trading desk on the stock exchange to specifically handle managed account trades. "We had to do our fixed income trades through the individual broker, but we did our equity trades through Hutton's trading desk," said Calamos. "The trades had to be called in individually."

By the late 80s, most firms had established their own trading desks for managed accounts. (See more about the development of technology in Chapter 8) This made doing business much easier for the money managers, because the new trading desks would handle the smaller order flow from the separate accounts, while the institutional desks would not. The new desks began doing block trades, then allocating the various trade sizes to the individual accounts at the end of the day. "We liked it because we got best execution when we did trades that way," said Gibb.

As more and more broker/consultants began doing the business, brokerage firms became much more organized internally. With more brokers at more firms participating and the development of technology as the 90s approached, the groundwork was laid for the early work of the independent money managers to become more lucrative.

DOING BUSINESS IN THE 'NEW ERA'

John Calamos recounted how business was developed in the early days. "Because of my experience as a stockbroker in the 70s, I was able to relate to the broker/consultant community and what they were trying to do there," explained Calamos. "As our institutional business developed and we began to be recognized in the convertible strategies area, we caught the attention of members of the broker/consultant community."

For a while, Calamos sat on the board of the IIMC (now IMCA) and spoke at some of the early conferences held by the organization. "Our approach was more of an educational one on why our strategy should be a part of their asset allocation," said Calamos. "There were very few—if any—investment firms in the early 80s that had any type of relationship with brokers," added Frank Gibb. Many relationships were developed through the consultant organizations, IMCA and IIMC. The early managers (like Calamos) were popular speakers at the IMCA and IIMC conferences. Networking was the name of the game and it was much easier to meet new broker/consultants in the educational environment.

Increasingly, more money managers began either to launch their own independent firms or to concentrate on SMAs as the concept of capturing more assets through broker/consultant relationships became popular. Brokers were looking for a better way to do business — a way to add value and eliminate conflicts of interest — and the new money management firms had the solutions. Hutton paved the way for the industry to provide those solutions.

The Hutton Select Managers program offered (in addition to Invesco, S&P, Calamos, Frontier, and Cap Guardian) such managers as Gardner Preston Moss and Provident Investment Counsel. Then State Street, Babson, NWQ, Palley Needleman, Rittenhouse, Munder, Dreman Capital, Callan, Roger Engemann, Nicholas-Applegate, 1838, Brandes Investment Partners, Lazard, Regent and others soon joined the movement and brought significant diversification among styles and disciplines. While many of the managers focused on institutions, some specialized in individual high net worth accounts.

Value and global manager, Brandes Investment Partners, targeted this market after founder Charles Brandes—a former broker—turned to portfolio management in the 70s. Said Director of Private Client Portfolio Management at Brandes, Bob Gallagher, "We didn't fully enter the institutional business until 1994, since we were concentrating on taking care of our affluent clients. To help grow our business, we developed many relationships in the early days with the pioneering consultants who researched and chose their own managers for their high level clients."

Ultimately, the market for this business proved to be fertile ground for Brandes and other managers, advisors, sponsors and, most importantly, very beneficial for investors.

SEPARATELY MANAGED ACCOUNTS

GROWTH—ESTABLISHED MANAGERS

Investment Manager AUM in SMAs

Source: MMI/FRC

"I received a call from the president of Shearson. He said, 'Your office is on the 102nd Floor of the WTC. Have your secretary pack up your office now and meet you there.' From that day forward, I never returned to the Hutton building."

—Peter Muratore, Chairman
MMI Board of Governors

Over the next decade, the foresight of the pioneers at Hutton spawned the cloning of new managed account business throughout the industry. The rapid growth in technology during the decade and the proliferation of wealth among high net worth individuals fueled the adoption of consulting platforms throughout the major broker-dealer firms, and then, in a different form, among the independent firms. By the end of the 80s, these developments laid significant groundwork for the swift growth of the industry during the 90s.

At Hutton, the Suggests programs One, Two, Three and Four were in full swing. Suggests One and Two were fee plus commission arrangements, with the fee covering the service portion of the contract and commissions covering the trade execution portion. Securities were custodied outside the firm. Two contracts were signed for each account, one with Hutton and one with the money manager. Suggests Three and Four saw the first all-inclusive fee arrangement, with custody either in-house or outside. The full menu of investment services was available including the writing of the investment policy statement (IPS), asset allocation, manager search and evaluation, and performance monitoring.

Through Suggests, Hutton took over the majority of the administrative functions in exchange for lower management fees and the reduction of account minimums to $250,000, then $100,000. Business streamed in and the managers became overwhelmed with the smaller accounts. As a result, managers began raising minimums again to $250,000, which spurred more brainstorming from the Hutton Consulting Group.

The Suggests program was still under a structure where, if a client wanted to fire a manager, Hutton would also suffer a breach of the relationship. During the late 70s and early 80s, the best an advisor/consultant could hope for—in terms of a relationship and ongoing compensation from a money manager—was to keep bringing the manager new business. Even then, consultant compensation usually ran for no more than a year on each new piece of business.

The consultants at Hutton wanted a way to receive ongoing compensation from the services they were providing these new clients. After all, they had freed the money manager of the bulk of the administrative and service functions on the account. The old payment structure simply was no longer valid. But the managers were certainly not going to initiate anything new that would change things.

In 1987, the pioneers initiated an extraordinary new program called Hutton Select Managers in which a client would sign only one contract – with Hutton. (See more on Hutton Select Managers in Chapter 8.) The money managers became subadvisors of the firm, so if a client wanted to fire a manager, it no longer meant they fired Hutton as well. Hutton simply conducted a search for a new manager and maintained the relationship with the client. Hutton was now in a position to insist on an ongoing share of compensation and there was little the managers could say about it. Fence-riding time was over for the managers – they were either in on the new industry, or they weren't.

According to Peter Muratore, "When Hutton first established their programs, every manager who joined was required to sign an exclusivity agreement with Hutton, so they couldn't manage money for other companies. OpCap was the only one who had maintained that exclusivity long-term."

Jim Lockwood retired from Hutton in 1987, about the time Hutton Select was launched, to enjoy more time with his wife, Audrie, and their six children.

Other Firms Want In

Two things were unique about this decade – technological development and product diversification within the industry. Pension funds were quickly growing from contributions and hefty market returns, making a greater need for diversification among managers readily apparent. Larger independent consultants were forcing money managers to further define their investment process, which meant having a universe of stocks from which to choose, and a disciplined buy and sell process. If a firm demonstrated a history of doing these things consistently with consistent results, it generally won the competition for significant funds.

The genius of the Hutton Select structure lay in the fact that through their consulting services, they could now lock in continuing commissions from a referred manager for the life of the relationship. Naturally, other firms decided they wanted a share of this business. Believers in the "new industry" chose to build their own platforms, while non-believers thought the new way of doing business would never last and declined to enter the arena.

Said Len Reinhart, "This was about the time Merrill, Prudential, and Paine Webber decided to enter the business. They dabbled in it earlier, but when they saw Select Managers and the success of that program, they started thinking seriously about the business. It was the spring of 1987, perfect timing for the market crash!! They tried to mimic the Select program and that's when the business really took off. On one hand we thought, 'now we will really have a lot of competition,' but on the other hand we were doing more business than we had ever done before. The competition actually helped fuel the advisor interest as well as the investor interest, making it more acceptable to do the business."

In Dick Schilffarth, the believers got a lot of help from one of the original Hutton pioneers. He left Hutton in 1983 to form his own firm, Richard Schilffarth and Associates (RS&A). "It was a consulting company," said Schilffarth, " and our job was to create managed asset departments in regional and national brokerage firms and to consult with investment managers on the possibility of becoming wrap account managers."

Firms clamored at Schilffarth's door. Many of the large firms were distancing themselves from oil and gas and real estate limited partnership business after due diligence proved many of them to be unworkable or concluded the general partner lacked experience. The managed account industry was ready to provide a custom solution for many investors' needs at the time (with attractive tax implications), and RS&A was there every step of the way to guide the advisors who wanted to learn more.

RS&A developed a platform and a training program whereby the firms could quickly create their own programs by using Schilffarth's tools. RS&A became the consultant on the Managed Assets Consulting (MAC) program at Prudential, then followed with PaineWebber, Wheat First, Legg Mason, Tucker Anthony, Sutro, Boettcher, Underwood Neuhaus, Scott and Stringfellow, Janney Montgomery Scott, Dain Bosworth and other programs. According to Schilffarth, these programs differed very little from the Hutton programs. "We had a product manager and a program that included the ability to produce an investment plan, find appropriate managers and have a quarterly report afterwards," he explained.

But Schilffarth also had training programs for brokers, teaching them how to market the new style of doing business and how to handle the functions of being a consultant. The firms began to make their own agreements with Schilffarth's managers and set up their own universes with managers and subcontractors.

The independents of the decade didn't have the capital to buy into the platforms required to use individual managers or the ability to do equities, so they used what they knew — mutual funds — to develop their own version of the wrap program. This development was largely responsible for the rapid growth of the mutual fund industry during the late 80s.

According to Chip Roame, Managing Principal, Tiburon Strategic Advisors, the independent advisors became masters at the consulting process because they had no variety of product to offer clients other than mutual funds. "They did financial planning right up front, getting the right asset allocation, picking the right mutual fund – it was always about that process," said Roame.

Their ranks developed as a result of the bank mergers that occurred, displacing a lot of trust officers, who subsequently decided to open up their own shops. Said Kevin Keefe, an analyst at Financial Research Corporation (FRC), "You had the RIA community primarily wrapping no-loads and the wirehouses with the separate accounts. By 1989, the investing public had begun to understand the new mutual fund wrap product and the broad-based financial press was touting its benefits as well. Add to that the high rate of adoption of qualified plans and the subsequent inclusion of mutual funds in those plans, and it's easy to see how the growth of the fund industry proliferated."

By this time, interest in the managed account business as a whole was catapulting. Schilffarth began consulting with the likes of Oppenheimer Capital and John Templeton's program, then called University Portfolio Management (Templeton Portfolio Management today). Rittenhouse, a newly formed venture by George Canell and Bernie Frances, soon set up their own account manager with Schilffarth's help. Schilffarth's firm then generated the idea of setting up a training program for brokers to become fully discretionary managers in their own right.

Some firms balked at joining the party early on. Many money managers felt they had a lock on their institutional accounts with a firm. But as consultants began calling on them and offering the new services, the consultant could be fired if they didn't fit the objectives of the client or did not perform adequately. Dean Witter and other firms were hesitant to welcome the new consulting relationships into their business model for fear of losing high dollar institutional business that was already established. "They saw the consultants developing a business they believed was interfering with the institutional money managers who were placing trades with the institutional brokers at the firm," explained First Union's

Dan Bott. (See Chapter 3 for more information.)

But many firms later realized the valuable opportunity they had passed up, including Merrill, who came back to the table in 1987 with its own program called 'Consults.'

The Consults program was not simply a copycat of the Hutton program. At Merrill, clients would enter a sort of tri-party agreement, as opposed to the two-party agreement structure that Hutton had established. "The client would sign one contract with Merrill to provide a service and another directly with the money manager. Then Merrill would sign a contract with the money manager to provide its services to the Consults program," said Alan Sislen, President, Managed Account Perspectives, and former head of managed accounts at Merrill Lynch.

According to Sislen, Merrill Lynch had been a big player in the performance measurement side of the business for institutional accounts since 1967. This service was primarily provided to large pension plans, endowments and foundations. In the mid-80s, Merrill sold that business, but still had the capability and the staff who understood the money manager side of the managed accounts industry. So Merrill still had the ability to provide the service to small institutions and to retail clients.

Merrill subsequently added other services to their well-established performance reporting program, such as a fact-finding questionnaire, a roster of money managers, trading capability, and other services necessary to operate in the separate account world. As a result, Consults was born.

The firm felt that their separate account clients were equally clients of the money managers. The money managers were required to keep their own records, to review the contract for suitability and to decide if they wanted to work with that client. Consults clients primarily kept in contact with their Merrill advisor, but if they had a question for the money manager, they had direct access to that money manager. Merrill's program was the only program at the time that allowed clients to have this direct access.

Merrill did set up a separate accounts trading desk within the Consults program, but the other administrative duties were duplicated between the systems. Security APL was formed and Merrill became one of its biggest customers, because it was the only software at the time that really focused on the managed accounts business. Merrill would set up the entire account on their system, using APL, then send it to the money manager to set everything up on whatever system they were using. The managers would send out

Another distinguishing factor in the Consults program was the small number of managers allowed into the program. This was by design, in order to help the manager gather more assets. Even today, Merrill's Consults program has the smallest number of managers of any of the major sponsors. All of the managers in the Consults program, however, were also in the programs of the other major sponsors. At that time, it was prudent for managers to be a part of as many programs as possible in order to gain leverage.

THE GIANTS MERGE

Said Charlie Carroll, managing director of Lazard, LLC, and formerly with Shearson Asset Management, "Because Shearson was part of AMEX at that time, they had a number of asset management subsidiaries— Boston Company, then, after the merger, Hutton Investment Management, Hutton Directions, Capital Management and Shearson Asset Management. They were all competing for shelf space, not just against one another with their own in-house brokers, but also against all these asset managers that sat on the independent platforms. I think it was good for the in-house managers and the external managers because it widened the pool and made for a more competitive and Darwinian environment."

In 1986, Shearson Lehman Brothers launched their Portfolio Management programs which provided commission-based brokers the next step to offering managed accounts. The trading decisions were made by the analysts in New York. The few advisors accepted into the PM Program had full discression on how they managed their client's portfolios. (Unlike in the Guided Portfolio Management program, launched in 1992, where the advisors had far less discression and had to choose from a list of securities recommended by the firm's research department — thus the term 'guided.')

Soon after, key execs were in serious discussions about acquiring Hutton—the immense talent and pool of business would be a feather in their cap. Approximately two years later, on April 29, 1988, the Shearson/Hutton merger was approved.

"It was as if a switch had been turned on," said Muratore. "Numerous firms, both large and small, decided they wanted into the business. Many of our people in the consulting area suddenly were being offered wonderful opportunities and large sums of money to leave Hutton and start up similar organizations in other firms. Amazingly, very few left at that time."

The rush of Shearson to become a major player in the business was demonstrated by a call received on the day of the buyout of Hutton. Said Muratore about his personal experience with the merger, "The day Shearson took over Hutton in 1988, I received a phone call at 9 a.m. from the president of Shearson. He said, 'Your office is on the 102nd floor of the World Trade Center. Have your secretary pack up your office and meet you there. You leave right away.' From that day forward, I never returned to the Hutton building."

Muratore said that a number of key individuals left Shearson soon after the merger. He stayed on for about 18 months, after which time he became president of Oppenheimer Capital Distributors.

At the time, Shearson had a private client group with a managing board of seven members: Hardwick ("Wick") Simmons was chairman of the group, which included four members each from Hutton and Shearson. Shearson had a much smaller program, and since Hutton's consulting program was the stronger of the two, it survived the merger. Hutton's direct investment and insurance products also survived the merger, as did Shearson's mutual funds.

Shearson introduced its TRAK program in 1989. TRAK, the first mutual fund wrap program, was the evolution of separately managed accounts in a mutual fund format. Said MFS' Bob Leo, "I was made director of mutual funds about that time, and even though I got a lot of credit for TRAK, it was Len Reinhart's innovation.

One of my colleagues, Marty Phillips, took it from concept to building the program at that time. He took it to about $10 billion by the mid-90s." Leo left Shearson in 1994 for MFS Investment Management.

THE NEED FOR TRAINING BIRTHS INDUSTRY ASSOCIATIONS

Training in the new business platform became a critical need so that the new consultants could be fully equipped to deliver the new service package in a professional, credible fashion. Certain forward-thinking individuals also saw organizational support as an integral ingredient in the long-term success of the managed account concept. Certified Financial Planners had an organization for their side of the industry, and Certified Public Accountants had an organization for theirs as well. So, Dan Bott decided it was time to create an organization to provide initial and continuing education for brokers to be trained in the new business of consulting.

First, the exact market the organization was to serve had to be identified. "I suggested that we needed to be more visionary, look out into the next decade and ask ourselves, 'Is this profession going to evolve?' There were a lot of people in the mid-80s who didn't think it would. The few who did were in the minority," said Bott.

Bott, along with colleague Jim Owen, then marketing chief at NWQ Investment Management in Los Angeles, developed business plans and marketing strategies, and in 1985 launched the Investment Management Consultants Association (IMCA). That first year, membership grew at a slow but steady pace, yet Bott grew increasingly dissatisfied with the direction IMCA was taking.

"I felt that the organization was putting up barriers of entry to those brokers who needed remedial training so they could go to the next level and eventually become consultants," said Bott. "It served the branch-based institutional consultant, though, very well and did a lot for legitimizing the middle market. I just had a different vision, that's all. Soon, I left IMCA and developed a plan to launch a learning institute designed to educate, train and designate any broker who wanted to become more professional and learn the investment process to better serve their clients."

After he left IMCA, Bott put in long hours before and after work and on weekends to form a new organization. With the help of long-time friend, Jack Polley (who passed away in 1997) of National Education Corporation, Bob Wood, Director of Marketing for Brandes Investment Partners (also passed away), and a number of other brokers who volunteered their time, the new organization began to take shape.

By 1988 the Institute for Investment Management Consultants (IIMC) was formed, offering a professional designation— Certified Investment Management Consultant (CIMC)— for those who desired to add credibility to their new function as well as a way for consultants to come together and decide how they would differentiate themselves in this new industry. Bott so believed in the concept of education, he invested his own capital to keep the organization afloat until it began creating its own revenues through conferences, designation courses, and audiotapes.

Said Bott, " In 1988, with the help of our new executive director—my friend, Jim Johnson—we launched the CIMC program. There were about a dozen charter members who received the Charter Member recognition as the first Certified Investment Management Consultants through the Institute, including John Gepfert, Jim Suellentrop, Anthony Lotruglio, Bert Meem, Ephraim Ulmer, and Tom Clark.

After receiving strong encouragement from the industry to merge associations, in March 2002 the Institute joined forces with the Investment Management Consulting Association (IMCA) to further expand its capabilities to provide consultants a source for increasing their knowledge and expertise in the consulting side of the industry. (See Chapter 12 for more information on education.)

What Characterized the 80s?

With the encroachment of discount brokerage on the industry

(e.g., Schwab, Jack White), vision and creativity were critically needed now. Soon, innovations in technology shone an even brighter light on managed accounts and enabled advisors and their firms to better compete in a commission-embattled marketplace.

"The 80s were a very creative period," said Gerald Bott, Vice President at Merrill Lynch's Jacksonville, Fla. office, and Dan Bott's brother. Previously at Kidder Peabody, Jerry Bott was primarily responsible for Kidder's entrance into the managed money arena. He left the production world in the early 70s, and after a brief respite, went back into production in 1980.

"I had five or six relationships that had stayed with me ever since I started in the business in 1966," said Bott. "I asked myself, 'why did these people stay with me all this time?'" Bott discovered that the accounts had two things in common: First, third party managers managed five of the six. Second, he communicated with them on a regular basis. When he realized this, he also recognized that, in order to truly accommodate clients using the investment process, more training and support were needed by the firm. After Bott spearheaded an effort at Kidder, two years later, in 1982, a consulting division was created.

As excellent testimony to the value of managed accounts and consulting, Bott captured large assets as he continued to educate clients about their benefits. Clients were satisfied with his level of service and put their trust in him and the managers he chose. Bott said, "By 1984, I had $1 billion of assets under consulting contracts and was generating some strong six figures [in gross production]." He broke the seven-figure mark in 1987, a year not fondly remembered by the industry.

Seamless Integration Begins

Technology was another powerful, characterizing force in the 80s. The personal computer (PC) began taking hold and provided much more capability for carrying out the services needed for the consulting industry. Many firms, up until the mid-80s or so, primarily provided performance reporting. Later in the decade, the continuing improvements in the PC and software enabled a full range of services to be provided to clients. "We worked with Bob Padgette at the firm and he took the process and the software and made it 100 times better by giving us the ability to maintain databases, and do better performance reports and other functions so important to the client," said Jerry Bott.

Padgette left Kidder in 1989 to start his own software provider company, Mobius Group. The success he'd had at Kidder creating software for the various functions of the consulting process — a manager database, performance reporting, financial planning, and asset allocation — made his company a major player in the development of technology for the new industry.

It was also during this decade that Security APL founder and Osprey Partners president Jay Whipple III made it possible to create smooth integration between the various functions required to run separately managed accounts. Whereas Padgette's Mobius provided technology for front-office functions, Security APL provided technology for the back-office and workflow connectivity.

CheckFree purchased Security APL in 1996 and Mobius Group in 1999. CheckFree provided what would be called "middle-office" functions such as trade execution and reconciliation. The marriage of the three was a significant step in the effort towards seamless integration. All three separate services sprang from the 1980s, spurred by the advent of the desktop computer and the ability to create spreadsheets, accurately compute returns and standard deviations (investment volatility and risk), and make impressive graphics.

Combined with the proliferation of new product, this development catapulted the industry into the 90s, a period where gathering significant market share was the name of the game – climaxing a series of events that would mold the industry into what it is today.

"Two-thirds of the firms out there today, begrudgingly, started to embrace it because it became an alternative to going out of business."

— Daniel R. Bott, Sr. CIMC, Managing Director
Bott & Associates, Investment Consulting Group
First Union Securities

To grow market share, wise and talented money managers stepped up their marketing efforts in the 80s and 90s to reach sponsor firms. During this decade, managed account platforms were being developed by such third-party providers as Lockwood Financial, Brinker, Portfolio Management Consultants (PMC), London Pacific Advisors, and SEI, to name a few of the earliest entrants. Brokerage firms were consolidating, and banks and insurance companies were acquiring respected regional firms.

Then in the mid-to-late 90s, a steady number of brokers decided to make the sometimes-difficult transition from commission-based business to fees. This decade also saw Schwab introduce OneSource, the first mutual fund marketplace, in 1992.

The development of sub-advisory fee programs (brokerage firm agreements with outside money managers) began to unfold and the institutional business was evolving with very little interference from the institutional trading desks. The 90s also witnessed an industry surge in targeting affluent markets, as intergenerational money and the transfer of trillions of dollars spotlighted baby boomers.

The industry was reeling from the evolution it was experiencing.

FIERCE COMPETITION

Competition was looming as discount brokers, online trading, and websites offering basic money management services gave the industry an abrupt wake-up call. According to Angie Clark, National Sales Manager, Pimco/Allianz Investments, "The most drastic evolution I saw throughout the 90s was that the minimum account size and the fees decreased. The broker training and support increased to the sponsor firms, as well as the caliber of marketing materials and value-added communication tools. Those were the most important changes I've seen in the last 12 years, and today that support is accelerating."

Said Len Reinhart about the encroachment, "I saw something changing—it was the competition. It used to be that one of our brokers [at Hutton] would call one of us in the Group and say, for example, 'I'm up against Merrill Lynch. What should I do?' Now brokers say, 'I'm up against a CPA, I think, and he's selling no load funds at Schwab.' You couldn't really put your finger on who the competition actually was at that time."

Feeling the effects of competitive recruitment activity, one by one, firms began developing their consulting departments. Said Dan Bott, "If they didn't have a department in place by 1995, they couldn't recruit good top brokers, and if the broker had 10-25% of their business in managed accounts, the firms didn't have much to offer that broker. Many firms who didn't want in on the business early only got in later because they were losing some of the big accounts to those who had managed account and consulting programs—or they would lose a broker who joined a competitor."

During the second half of the 90s, enough big managed account business was showing up that firms recognized it as not only a viable revenue source, but also as a valuable service to investors. It was a business they wanted to embrace as an innovative financial solution for clients. Since numerous traditional brokerage products were now being sold through multiple channels, the competitive pricing structures brought the margins down. In 1998, when the industry began to feel the powerful sting of online trading and full-service broker commissions were affected, most firms realized that fee-based business would eventually be in their future.

Fee-based revenue attached to the growth of assets was very stable. It looked like it was going to be a mainstay. Bott affirmed, "Two-thirds of the firms out there today, begrudgingly, started to embrace it because it became an alternative to going out of business." Far-sighted clearing firms (those that hold assets and perform other services for small-to mid-sized broker-dealers) entered the business because they, too, saw the value to investors as well as the potential of retaining and recruiting brokers and advisors.

Shearson Folds in Hutton

After Shearson Lehman purchased Hutton in 1987, the firm became known as Shearson Lehman Hutton under the management of chairman Peter Cohen. Len Reinhart recounted some dissatisfaction with management soon after Hutton was taken over, "It was my belief that management viewed us as a cash cow," said Reinhart. "They started cutting our expenses even though our business was growing 35% a year. I began functioning more as an administrator putting out fires and negotiating for our group than as a consultant."

There was quite a bit of infighting over which managers they could hire and fire, he added. "Once we fired Salomon Brothers—before the merger, of course—but the head of trading was upset because our group had just cost the trading department one of their biggest clients," said Reinhart. " Even though we won more often than we lost, it was a constant battle."

Reinhart resigned in 1995, and in 1996 launched Lockwood Financial named after his friend and mentor, the late Jim Lockwood. Currently his firm provides independent advisors with managed account platforms similar to those he created for Hutton and SSB.

Mutual Fund Wraps: Competition for Separately Managed Accounts?

In 1998, Cerulli Associates conducted industry research on whether mutual fund wrap programs retained investor assets longer than traditional mutual funds. The study concluded that cash flow in the brokerage mutual fund wrap programs was less volatile. Qualified plan assets comprised about half of the assets in these programs, which greatly aided their stability.

During the four years from 1993-1997, the average annual growth of mutual fund wrap programs was 76%, while the separately managed account programs (then called wrap accounts) lagged by 22% due to the investing public's familiarity with mutual fund investing and the industry's aggressive marketing.

Cerulli found another reason investors were looking beyond mutual funds was poor performance. In the 90s, all but a few funds trailed the Standard & Poor's 500, so investors began looking elsewhere. Some were trading online, but the wealthier investors were counseled by wise advisors who saw the power of separately managed accounts and began using them for their high-net-worth clients.

One attractive benefit of these accounts was the tax advantages. According to Reinhart, in 1998 funds made taxable distributions amounting to 12% of assets. For an investor with $1 million in funds, that would have been $120,000 in distributions. "Even if those were all long-term capital gains," said Reinhart, "the investor would have paid $24,000 in taxes. In contrast, some independent managers delivered a 20% average return on separate accounts without triggering capital-gains taxes, by pairing off losses with gains."

In 1997, there were approximately 70 mutual fund wrap programs offered by at least 60 sponsors, compared with 25 managed account programs offered by 22 sponsors. Smith Barney was the leader in fund wraps with an asset share of 19%, followed by Merrill Lynch with 13% and SEI with 11%. Even though the assets were growing faster at regional broker-dealers, wirehouses still controlled the largest share, for a total of 40%.

The median account minimum for separately managed account programs was $100,000, while the mutual fund wrap median was $50,000. By year-end 1997, assets in separately managed account programs totaled $220 billion, according to figures compiled by the Money Management Institute (MMI), the national organization for the separately managed account industry.

About the same time, Schwab began providing financial advisors access to 34 private account managers through its new program, Schwab Managed Account Connection. They used such managers as Lazard, State Street and Warburg. Its minimums were $250,000. Third-party providers PMC and Lockwood offered $100,000 minimums at that time.

In 1992, Shearson Lehman launched their Guided Portfolio Management (GPM) programs, giving the brokers less discretion over investor portfolios (See Chapter 5 for more information). By the mid-90s, Smith Barney was a market leader in separately managed accounts. By 1999, they claimed more than $60 billion in SMAs, catapulting them to the number one position in the industry with the most assets in that product group.

Said Reinhart, "During that period of time the managed account sales slid off a bit – not that they declined in size but they were not growing as fast because a lot of the attention was going to the mutual fund wraps. Then, around 1996, investors began to get a little bit disenchanted with mutual funds. They began to realize they couldn't control the taxable outcome, and their total return was being dramatically impacted by taxes. Soon managed accounts appealed to a wide audience of affluent investors because the firms could efficiently run after-tax accounts using the evolving technologies."

Mutual Fund Encroachment

When the fund companies saw a slowdown in net inflows to their funds, they began to appreciate the potential for separately managed accounts to produce large asset gains— despite some of the unique difficulties of doing SMA business. In order to compete with the brokerage houses, they seriously considered launching their own SMA products and an entirely new team of wholesalers to sell managed accounts,

They realized quickly that working in the separately managed accounts sector required a more knowledgeable sales force who could discuss the investment process, not just performance. As a result, many fund companies today are hiring industry trainers and coaches to train their regional sales representatives, and a number of firms are re-naming their sales forces: Senior VPs, Managed Account Consultants, Managed Account Analysts and so on.

Industry researcher, TowerGroup, reported that large fund firms like Scudder were training and supporting advisors, bringing their brand name to investors who previously had no experience with managed accounts. Tower's research also pointed out that this action on the part of the funds should prompt brokerage firms to bring pricing closer to that of funds, which would increase investor demand for managed accounts.

Ever-increasing demands then led to the 1990 establishment of the Association for Investment Management and Research (AIMR), the worldwide, non-profit organization of more than 50,000 investment practitioners and educators in more than 100 countries. AIMR educates and examines investment managers and analysts, and helps sustain high standards of professional conduct. The organization was created from the merger of the Financial Analysts Federation (FAF) that was founded in 1947, and the Institute of Chartered Financial Analysts (ICFA) that was founded in 1959.

SAYING "GOODBYE" TO A LEGEND

Amidst all of the activity in this decade, some of the early pioneers were retiring, more advisors were becoming consultants, and droves of commissioned brokers were successfully transitioning to fee business. Sadly, Jim Lockwood passed away in 1994 (he retired from Hutton in 1987 before the merger), having prepared thousands of advisors to follow in his footsteps. According to Lockwood's widow, Audrie, before he retired Hutton offered him a $5 million retirement bonus, but he turned it down saying he wouldn't take a penny of shareholders' money. This was a last great testimony to a man with the highest of ethical standards. The industry mourned his death, but celebrated his contributions.

John Ellis, who succeeded Lockwood as manager of the Consulting Group, said, "Jim had the greatest leadership qualities of any person I have ever known. He was to the investment industry what Vince Lombardi was to football." Ellis retired from Shearson Lehman Bros in 1992, before the Salomon Smith Barney merger, turning the reins over to Len Reinhart.

Sources: Financial Research Corporation (FRC); Cerulli Report, "Understanding the Wrap Market, November 1998; TowerGroup, "Replacing Funds in the New Millennium, May 2001; BusinessWeek, November 1999 "So Long Glory Days"

"Mutual funds have lost assets, and have shrunk considerably in that time [two years]. What's incredible is that separately managed accounts have done exactly the opposite."

— Kevin Keefe, Senior Analyst
Financial Research Corporation (FRC)

1   The Current Environment

In early 2002, total assets in separately managed accounts grew faster than any other mainstream financial services product, and rapidly were closing in on much more established retail financial services products. A newly featured program, the multiple style account, which packages several investment styles in one account (and often with lower investment minimums), began to blossom throughout the industry.

According to the Money Management Institute, industry-wide assets in separately managed accounts approached $416 billion at the mid point of 2002.

By mid 2002, a prestigious group of 10 asset managers accounted for approximately 35% of all consultant-managed assets. Citigroup Asset Management continued its lead—in terms of assets under management—of all managers participating in consultant managed account programs. Others in the top 10 category, as reported by Cerulli Associates in late 2002, are Brandes Investment Partners, Nuveen Rittenhouse, Regent Investor Services, 1838 Investment Advisors, Rorer Asset Management, Lazard Asset

Management, Lord Abbett, TCW Investment Management, and Laurel Capital Advisors. As a proprietary manager, Citigroup's Private Portfolio Group manages assets in their Consulting and Evaluation Services (CES) and Fiduciary Services (FS) platforms, but a much larger $60 billion flows directly from SSB advisors.

Peter Cieszko, Managing Director and head of their U.S. retail and high net worth group, said the Citigroup programs are a roll-up of Smith Barney Asset Mgmt., Salomon Asset Management, and the old Citibank Asset Management. They continue to use Salomon Bros. Asset Management as their third-party brand for distribution outside of their proprietary channels.

Financial Research Corporation (FRC) reported in a recent study, *Best Practices in the Separately Managed Account Industry*, that the big five New York wirehouses (Salomon Smith Barney, Merrill Lynch, Morgan Stanley Dean Witter, PaineWebber, and Prudential) controlled 70% of the managed account market by 2001. But this business is being encroached upon as banks, regional brokerages, and third-party vendors (i.e., Lockwood, Brinker Capital and Wells Fargo) have made inroads.

Plus, there is a growing number of these third-party, separately managed account programs being offered by organizations without a captive distribution force, reported FRC. These programs rely predominantly on business from financial advisors not affiliated with a major distributor, including Registered Investment Advisors (RIAs.)

Said Dick Schilffarth, "I believe that the third-party managed account provider market is getting overcrowded. When I was providing the service, there were only four of us in the business: myself with Portfolio Consulting Services, Portfolio Management Consultants, Brinker, and Len Reinhart with Lockwood. Today, I can pay $5,000 for a program called Investor Force that allows me to search a universe of 1,000 money managers and 200 hedge managers, and it has a quarterly report package in it." According to a recent survey from Tiburon Research, on January 1, 2002, there were approximately 50 turnkey asset management providers (TAMPs), a category that includes online services.

SIGNIFICANT CHANGES

After nearly three decades of slow, but steady, growth, why all the recent attention toward this business? Experts say advisors are witnessing the success their colleagues are having with managed accounts and they are eager to provide value-added solutions, too. They want to "sit on the same side of the table" with their clients, offer real benefits, and differentiate themselves from their competition in more professional ways. Brokerage firms—national and regional alike—are finally realizing it is the wave of the future and are now aggressively promoting various types of fee based business. They also want to avoid any compensation conflicts of interest.

SEPARATELY MANAGED ACCOUNTS

GROWTH PROSPECTS—DISTRIBUTORS

Rep Population Doing SMA Business

77%

38%

2001   2004E

Source: MMI/FRC

On May 19, 1994, the SEC released findings of the "Large Firm Report," led by Merrill's Chairman Dan Tully and his Blue Ribbon Commission. The Committee included Warren Buffett, Chairman and CEO of Berkshire Hathaway, and former Chairman of Salomon Brothers; Jack Welch, Chairman and CEO of General Electric; Raymond Mason, Chairman and CEO of Legg Mason; Sam Hayes, a noted Harvard Business School professor; and Tom O'Hara, Chairman of the National Association of Investors Corp. Said former SEC Chairman Arthur Levitt, "The Committee's mission was to identify industry compensation practices that raised significant conflicts of interest between registered representatives and customers, and to suggest ways to eliminate or reduce these conflicts."

Tully, in the report given to then-SEC Chairman Levitt, said, "The prevailing commission-based compensation system inevitably leads to conflicts of interest among parties involved. Full disclosure of conflicts of interest is important when dealing with investment professionals. However, understanding the impact of these conflicts is equally important; understanding who is truly working on the investors' behalf and who has an ax to grind."

The Commission conducted two national investigations with the self-regulatory organizations and state regulators, and took strong action where deficiencies were found. The industry developed and instituted a continuing education program for brokers, and encouraged a fresh look at how compensation can put brokers at odds with their customers' best interests. As a result, the commission issued a series of "best practices" for the industry to aspire to, which also included looking at fee-based compensation.

DRIVERS OF GROWTH

The drivers of separately managed account growth are many, including the following as reported by TowerGroup:

- Total fees for managed accounts used to be as high as 3% but have rapidly fallen to an average range of 1.8-2.0%. This has created much greater interest but, at the same time, has placed significant pressure on investment management firms. With the recent emergence of low-cost managed account programs like Schwab's 1% all-in-one platform, industry leaders like Merrill Lynch, Citigroup, and Morgan Stanley have been forced to revisit fees for their programs and average total fees paid by inventors for managed accounts.

- A significant increase in the number of high net worth investors has helped fuel separately managed accounts. The VIP Forum and Tiburon Research report that as of 2001, more than 8 million households have a net worth greater than $1 million. That number compares with only 2.3 million households in 1992, with the number of high net worth households growing at a 20% annual rate over the past eight years.

- With tax year 2000 as a backdrop, the argument for tax efficient investing has never hit closer to home for U.S. investors. The reality of having to write a check to the IRS for capital gains taxes on a mutual fund that provided zero return has motivated more and more investors to seek products that have the potential to provide a higher level of personal tax efficiency than mutual funds.

- Another key reason separately managed accounts have gained in popularity is the ongoing sophisticated due diligence (research and evaluation) process used by program sponsors to select and monitor the managers they offer to clients. Managers undergo complete examination and analysis by large numbers of highly trained individuals at the sponsoring firms. It includes investigation of portfolio managers, staff, investment performance, and the complete infrastructure of the firm. This process ensures that the managers chosen are appropriate and align with the client's goals, and continue to be in accordance with the investment policy statement (statement of client's goals, risk tolerance, etc.)

- New technologies and operational improvements have dramatically improved the efficiency of administering and managing these products. This has allowed investment managers and program sponsors to substantially lower account minimums from the $1 million-plus range to a distinctly more reachable $100,000 –150,000. These much lower investment thresholds have opened up separately managed accounts to a whole new group of potential clients.

Another significant driver is the positive publicity about managed accounts in the mainstream media. FRCs Kevin Keefe said,

SEPARATELY MANAGED ACCOUNTS

CONSULTANT SMA USAGE
Consultant AUM in SMAs

40% — 2001
49% — 2002E
61% — 2004E

Source: MMI/FRC

"Publications in the broad financial press like *Money, Fortune, Business Week* and *The Wall Street Journal* are devoting more coverage to the topic, which helps promote interest in managed accounts." Dan Bott agreed, "Today, we liken our position to 1991, when the retail firms were just recognizing the managed account business. We are now seeing the rest of the industry, the media, and a diverse group of investors waking up and recognizing it, too."

Merrill Lynch's Russell Smith, National Director of Sales and Marketing, agrees. Because of the increased recognition of separate accounts by the press, "Today's clients are more comfortable with investments and they are mentally prepared for something more challenging. The learning curve was slow in the 70s and the 80s, but it took off in the 90s. The learning curve is actually shortening regarding the acceptance of separately managed money. The support clients get from advisors and the dynamics of the environment are causing this."

Improved Technology

Arguably, technology is the single most important driver supporting the growth of separate accounts, as cited in FRCs "Best Practices" report. Automation of major portions of the management and administration of separate accounts has lowered the cost of maintaining and participating in such programs. This has allowed program sponsors and investment managers to steadily lower the minimum account sizes that will be accepted while at the same time lowering the average total fees charged to the end investor.

Given these dynamics, mutual fund companies, insurance companies, financial supermarkets like Schwab, Fidelity, and TDWaterhouse, accounting firms, and banks are either in the managed account market now, or are planning to enter it in the near term. But the expense and scale needed to start up and operate the business can be a major roadblock.

"Scale is a big question," said Chuck Widger, President and Chief Executive Officer of Brinker Capital. "Setting up an efficient, successful back office is tremendously difficult. Scalability on the front end is very important, as is technology to do it. Scale is also important with managed accounts because of the attention that each investor requires. Since it's a consultative sale and not a commodity, firms need to build in flexibility for the client."

Managed Accounts: Multiple Solutions Whose Time Has Come

FRC's Kevin Keefe explained that while we can blame the markets for some of the asset contraction in mutual funds, the gains that managed accounts have accomplished are somewhat at the expense of the fund industry. "The last two years have certainly convinced me that we are at a very important time in the retail investment product arena," said Keefe. "Mutual funds have lost assets, and have shrunk considerably in that time. What's incredible is that separately managed accounts have done exactly the opposite."

Keefe went on to explain that the high rate of adoption of funds in qualified plans and the transition from defined benefit to defined contribution retirement plans was a significant influence in the growth of the fund industry. The pension and retirement industry is witnessing parallels to the managed account business–the asset levels are similar and investors seem to be as interested and excited about managed accounts as they were about mutual funds in the late 80s-mid 90s. Said Keefe, "Other factors driving managed accounts also drove mutual funds. Many individuals are convinced that 401(k)s will have the option to place managed accounts in them. Operationally, it might be a challenge, but I believe they will, in fact, be available."

Keefe continued, "Distributors have been pushing managed accounts for a while; now the investment manufacturing firms are evaluating how the space is going to develop. I believe we will quickly see the industry develop a much more broad-based product. Minimums have come down, which has opened the door for a wide variety of investors, and the Multi-Discipline Products (MDPs)—or Multi-Discipline Accounts (MDAs) as some refer to them— should play a significant role in the industry if they are adopted on a broad basis. MDPs are bringing the concept to a wider audience, so that will certainly drive the industry going forward."

A recent white paper by FRC explains that while traditional managed account mandates cover a very finite piece of the investment universe — i.e., large cap growth U.S. equities — MDPs provide one-stop access to a broad swath of the investment universe. MDPs usually cover an entire capitalization or style category in one separately managed account 'vehicle.' Most MDPs contain at least three distinct sub-portfolios covering specific investment universes.

For example, U.S. Equity Large Cap is one of six strategies that the SSB Consulting Group offers though its new DSP (Diversified Strategic Portfolio) program. The strategy will cover the large cap growth, the large cap value and the large cap blend investment universes. The other DSPs follow core portfolio themes such as Global Balanced.

With investment minimums as low as $150,000, multiple discipline products offer the benefits of owning three or more traditional managed accounts with as little as $50,000 allocated to each sub-portfolio. MDPs have addressed one major challenge that managed accounts had when prospecting for lower-end investors— the challenge of diversification.

CitiGroup's Cieszko believes MDAs (MDPs) are the next wave in the managed account business for the high net worth investor. Citigroup is the pioneer of MDA accounts and owns the trademark on the name. "We have over $15 billion in just MDA products alone," he said. "We are able to customize accounts in over 200 ways for specific individuals, and have over 20 MDA models. Starting with a $100,000 minimum investment, clients will have one account that encompasses multiple investment disciplines. Each quarter, clients receive a Quarterly Review that consolidates all holdings and investment styles into one statement."

One of the biggest risks in the industry today is over-reliance by investors on a single manager, or a single style-specific allocation of assets. The MDA concept is refreshingly simple. Cieszko continued, "We are able take a minimum $100,000, and give half to large growth, half to large value. Or 40% large growth, 40% large value and 20% international. The secret is clients get one contract, one statement, one account, instant diversification, lower minimums and, most importantly, they're customized, so clients don't have overlapping securities."

With SSB's MDA success in 2001 and 2002, others are developing ways to enter the arena. AMG (Affiliated Managers Group) announced a new affiliated product and First Union has teamed up with them to offer Diversified Managed Allocation Portfolios using managers affiliated with AMG.

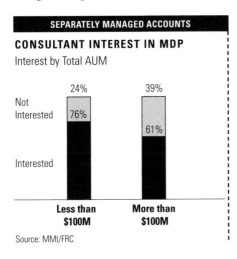

SEPARATELY MANAGED ACCOUNTS

CONSULTANT INTEREST IN MDP

Interest by Total AUM

Source: MMI/FRC

Keefe adds more of his own insight and offers another perspective on managed accounts, "Some advisors and investors will stick with mutual funds, and that's okay. There will always be a need for individuals who do the product sale better than the process sale. Advisors need to fully understand the benefits of MDPs and for which clients they are appropriate, instead of putting all the 'eggs in the MDP basket.'" He notices, however, that the higher up the asset ladder advisors climb, the less they tend to use packaged products. "It seems," he said, "at some point they began to push these products away and realize they just don't fit their world anymore. These advisors will either say, 'I work with MDPs' or 'I work with managed accounts.' But there's a program fit for everyone. Hopefully, distribution companies—which are very highly incented to get everyone on a fee-based program—will see it's not black OR white, it's black AND white."

WHAT'S THE *REAL* SCOOP ON MUTUAL FUND INVOLVEMENT?

While the mutual fund industry wrestles with the challenge of average redemption rates of more than 30% (at the time of this writing in the second quarter of 2002), managed account sponsors reported annual redemption rates as low as 8-10% and assets being held for an average of up to 10 years compared with three years in a mutual fund.

The terrific growth and a substantial existing asset base have brought a number of new entrants to the managed account field. Distributors such as Schwab have launched, or relaunched, proprietary separate account platforms, according to FRC.

"When I left SSB, 82% of all the brokers at SSB were using managed accounts in some way," said Schwab's Senior Vice President, Separate Accounts, Jeffrey Cusack, "and when I joined Schwab over two years ago, of the 6,000 advisors [firms and independents] who worked with Schwab, and over $300 billion total custodied, only 5% of them had ever opened a managed account with Schwab. Today, it's 15% overall, but if you look at the largest 1,000 of those advisors, about 31% have opened SMAs, and with the top 20, it's 70%. More than half of the assets are in Schwab Retail and there is certainly room for managed accounts in that mix. We have the Schwab Private Client offices, which is a full suite of services, and more relationship-based. We're developing the asset allocation, following up on the research and performance of the managers and monitoring—the investment process. So it's a deeper relationship with the client and it's a fee-based model. In Schwab Retail, though, we don't provide an overall fee-based offering."

Several fund companies like Invesco, Phoenix, and Rittenhouse have joined the ranks of established separate account investment managers. One of the more prominent entrants was AIM, the seventh-largest fund company in terms of long-term assets.

One fund group that has successfully tapped the managed account market is Phoenix Investment Partners, a diversified investment firm managing more than $60 billion in institutional and individual assets. They were among the first mutual fund companies to successfully make the transition from funds only to funds and managed accounts. Since strategically moving into managed accounts in 1995, this segment of Phoenix's business has prospered. Today, sales of sponsored managed accounts represent approximately 50% of Phoenix's retail sales volume.

Contributing further to its managed account growth, Phoenix was the first distributor of multiple money managers in this market and the forerunner of the industry trend toward aggregator models. From 1995 to date, Phoenix has expanded from a single money manager to eleven institutional-quality investment affiliates. As a result, Phoenix is ranked the second-largest holding company (multi-manager) of managed accounts, capturing a significant 3.6% of market share. But why the sudden interest by mutual fund companies?

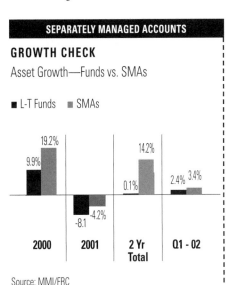

SEPARATELY MANAGED ACCOUNTS

GROWTH CHECK

Asset Growth—Funds vs. SMAs

■ L-T Funds ■ SMAs

Source: MMI/FRC

According to a Bernstein Research study, approximately $2 trillion of the $7 trillion in mutual funds is controlled by households with $1 million or more in total financial assets. Mutual fund executives have much to be concerned about, considering that nearly 30% of the assets in the industry are controlled by a group that is the key target of separately managed accounts—the wealthy. As more affluent investors are exposed to the benefits that managed accounts offer compared with traditional mutual funds, it may be just a matter of time before a shift of assets to managed accounts from existing mutual funds occurs. The study concluded that it is possible that an erosion of 25-50% of fund assets, equating to a shift of $500 billion - $1 trillion over the next 3-5 years, could occur.

Still, the escalating interest – and assets – are causing mutual fund companies to sit up and take notice. At the end of 2000, 45 firms offered both mutual fund asset management and separate account management via consultant-driven programs, according to the Money Market Directory (MMD), published by Standard & Poor's.

Some of these firms are mutual fund industry leaders, such as INVESCO, Janus, and Franklin Templeton. Others come from a more institutional background and offer mutual funds as a side business. These include such firms as Calamos Asset Management and Kayne Anderson Investment Management (purchased by Phoenix in 2002).

"I think that any mutual fund company that's a top 30 player needs to be looking very closely at this business," said Andrew Guillette, senior analyst at Cerulli Associates. "If a mutual fund company doesn't have an offering there, it just restricts asset growth."

Fund companies are definitely listening and are looking to acquire firms that manage separate accounts in order to add them to their lineup. Often, these are houses that have a strong institutional history, but little retail experience.

For example, in October 2001 S&P reported that Eaton Vance Corp. acquired majority stakes in two money managers with thriving separate accounts businesses with a total of about $8 billion in assets. The company first acquired 80% of Fox Asset Management for an initial payment of $32 million in cash and stock with up to $30 million in contingent future payments. It then bought 70% of Atlanta Capital Management Co. for $70 million in a similar deal. Nuveen made a very strategic purchase several years ago of Rittenhouse Financial, which by the end of 2001 had catapulted Nuveen into one of the top five positions in terms of assets under management in the coveted separate accounts universe before it was widely recognized as an important trend. Its recent acquisition of NWQ vaults its asset base higher.

Increasingly, fund companies are expanding management and salesforces in their existing separate accounts departments. In July 2001, Citigroup Asset Management, which controls over $60 billion in assets, scored big by naming Jamie Waller (formerly with CheckFree, and known for his brilliance in the area of technology and operations) director of managed accounts for the private portfolio group and third-party distribution.

Some mutual fund companies prefer to build their own separate accounts business from the bottom up. One such company is AIM Management Group. AIM's new subsidiary, AIM Private Asset Management, markets customized managed account portfolios to high net worth individuals and institutional markets.

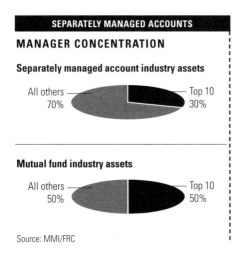

SEPARATELY MANAGED ACCOUNTS

MANAGER CONCENTRATION

Separately managed account industry assets

All others 70% — Top 10 30%

Mutual fund industry assets

All others 50% — Top 10 50%

Source: MMI/FRC

CPA firms are also entering the asset management business through such companies as PRIMA Capital and may prove to be serious competition and a potential roadblock for advisors seeking to network with centers of influence. Said Russ Prince of Prince and Associates, "I've seen some of the larger accounting firms get into the business in a big way. Some institutional consulting firms are actually moving into this business—those that were advising in the large plan sponsors and endowment funds."

THROUGH A VISIONARY'S EYES

Frank Campanale, a pioneer, and one of the financial services industry's forward-thinkers and innovators, looked back at the changes the industry has experienced over the past 25 years. "Our industry has gone from a transaction-based culture where stockbrokers were nothing more than merchants—selling products to clients— to a completely different mindset where, today, they are judged on their professionalism and how well they perform for the client in a fee-based world," he said

He continued, "The secret is to leverage our two most precious commodities: Our knowledge and our time. If a firm can leverage the FCs workday and make it easier for them to provide the highest level of service to the client, and get the fee down to something that's reasonable, everybody wins. And that's the environment we're all striving to create."

Sources: Financial Research Corporation (FRC); IMG/Thomson Financial, Thomson Financial/Investment Mktg Group; Financial Research Corporation (FRC); TowerGroup; Cerulli Associates; Money Management Institute; Bernstein Research

"We had an ash tray that made a great little pie chart. Then we progressed to a Radio Shack computer. Our first hard drive was an 8 megahertz — we thought that was really pretty fancy."

— John Brock, Sr. V.P., Investment Officer
Brock/Hazzard Investment Group
First Union Securities

8   THE VITAL ROLE OF TECHNOLOGY

The evolution of technology was a major factor in the continued advancement of the consulting industry. Development in the early days was slow. Platforms were crude and procedures for generating performance reports and other account management tools were long and arduous.

It was common business practice by the banks in the early 70s to keep performance information "close to the vest." Clients had confidence their money was being well managed simply because it was being held at a bank trust company, generating the assumption that the money was safe. Before this, very little information was given to the clients. They received reports, but clients had nothing against which to compare the performance of their accounts and no way of knowing which instruments or investment strategies were responsible for the performance generated.

The paper trail required by the Department of Labor with the advent of ERISA had to show investment guidelines and objectives, how advisory firms were selected and the type of monitoring being used to ensure the protection of the assets. To satisfy these requirements, many firms hired scores of accountants and financial officers to create reports and analyses—a complicated and expensive process. The development of suitable technology helped fiduciaries execute these responsibilities prudently by leveraging their time and money.

The First "Customizable Systems"

In these early days, firms such as Mercer and AG Becker created what was called a "black box" performance monitor that generated a thick book as a performance report. It was not customizable, so the client had no choice but to like what he or she received.

The first technology platforms used to generate customizable reports consisted of homemade scattergrams, according to Salomon Smith Barney's Frank Campanale. Top financial advisors began asking pension plan sponsors and wealthy individuals questions about their portfolio performance relative to the Dow Jones or the S&P 500. "Clients would get this kind of glazed look and admit they didn't know," said Campanale, "so, the first 'technology' was the creation of graphs and charts using color tape and those little Exacto knives."

Advisors began incorporating standard deviation to plot the risk and return characteristics of portfolios on the scatter diagrams. Standard deviation measurement was used to show how much risk a client was taking in order to achieve the performance generated. "It was a big revelation for many of these individuals to realize their portfolio was up 6.7% [within accepted standards at the time] but with 32% volatility," added Campanale. Thus, performance reporting really lit up the industry and the analytics of portfolios became important to institutional investors and wealthy individuals alike.

Transforming the Manager Relationship

When Len Reinhart joined the Hutton group in 1980 as an analyst, he began enhancing the Case system (named after creator George Case) to provide a more robust performance measurement system. In 1987, Hutton purchased a portfolio management record keeping system, the National Investor Data System (NIDS), developed by Carl Froebel. Before that time, money managers had to keep their own books and records as well as reconcile the figures to produce performance statements.

These functions were costly and required account minimums of $10 million to be feasible and clients signed contracts directly with the money manager. If the client had more than one account, he had to sign a separate agreement with each money manager, deal with a different pricing structure for each manager, and keep up with administrative functions for each account.

By the time account minimums reached the $500,000 mark, the money managers became inundated with smaller accounts and quickly reached critical mass. Hutton created an automated trading system that allowed managers to do block trades, then allocate the trades to the smaller portfolios at the end of the day. This enabled managers to lower minimums to $250,000, suddenly giving retail investors access to institutional quality money management for a single fee that included all transactions, all research, asset manager selection, performance analytics – an entire menu of services provided by the new broker consultants.

Reinhart was the point man behind the new trading system, implementing the back office functions (books, record keeping, etc.) of the NIDS system at Hutton, and tailoring the Case system for the more attractive front end (proposal generation, trading, performance reporting aspects) functions. This resulted in an entire shift in the separate accounts landscape - the formation of the Hutton Select Managers program. (See more on this in Chapter 5.)

Select Managers positioned the money manager as more of a subcontractor to the firm. Now, the managers worked for Hutton, who negotiated fees with the managers as a quantity purchaser, lowering account minimums and providing the back office support functions previously handled by the money managers.

This freed the managers to do what they did best, run portfolios. "Basically, we took over the client communication and all the administrative aspects of running the accounts," said Reinhart.

Clients could then sign one contract with Hutton and pick from 16 different money managers, all with the same fee structure. "We sort of went from a dirt road to a highway at that point," he added. "All of a sudden, we could process a lot more business and we could be a lot more competitive."

An avalanche of new, retail-sized accounts hit the firm and Select Managers had difficulty handling the increased volume because the proposal system was not scalable. Hutton revamped the business model and created the Smart System, which plugged right into Select Managers and gave it the ability to generate a massive amount of proposals and to handle the increase in accounts.

The First Computer-Based Technology

Toward the mid-80s, as money managers began migrating away from insurance companies and bank trust departments to set up their own operations, clients began to focus on performance relative to popular benchmarks. According to Citigroup's Jamie Waller, "There was a time in the late 70s when, if you did anything but buy the Dow, you outperformed it. So many of the managers had superior track records." Software firms began building performance measurement and trade modeling tools to cater to the newly independent managers.

According to Osprey's Jay Whipple, the first company to provide a service-driven solution to portfolio accounting was Bradford Trust Company. The system consisted of forms color-coded by type of transaction. The forms were mailed in and responses were received within two weeks – not very interactive, but it worked. Colleague Fred Towers then put the Bradford system on a Teletype machine. Transactions could then be input and portfolios could be generated.

During the early 70s Froebel, the real grandfather of modern portfolio accounting systems, created the most successful commercial portfolio accounting system at Advanced Data Processing Company (ADP). He then left, founded National Investor Data Systems (NIDS) and built the first stand-alone system that could be installed in an office.

Whipple began his career at the firm his grandfather and part-ner Bill Bacon had founded, Bacon Whipple. "I grew up with the brokerage business around the dining room table," he said. The firm had an outside service company that provided data feeds, which allowed Whipple to create a proprietary portfolio system for use at Bacon Whipple. He dreamed of a career going all the way to the top, but his dreams were cut short when another firm purchased Bacon Whipple. So Whipple hooked up with long-time friend Waller, took his portfolio accounting system with him and started Security APL just as the separate account business be-gan building. APL's target market became the independent money managers who left the insurance companies and bank trust de-partments to go out on their own. Some of these managers were included in Hutton's Suggest program.

Shortly after Whipple and Waller started APL, Bob Padgette, former Senior Vice President of CheckFree Investment Services, developed the Prime Consulting Group at Kidder Peabody. In early 1989, he left Kidder to found Mobius Group, first providing a manager database product, then following with performance re-porting, financial planning and asset allocation software. (Padgette is now retired.)

On the hardware side in the mid-80s, mainframes were still the primary data source. Security APL ran its programs on huge Digital Equipment Corporation mainframes, DEC 2060's. Shaw Data and NIDS were APL's main competitors at the dawn of the separately managed account industry. At many points along the way, the advancement of the industry truly led the development of the technology needed to support it, based on general technol-ogy available at the time. APL created the first scaled trade rebal-ancing function in answer to the industry's need for a scalable model to be applied to multiple accounts with sensitivity restric-tions. This was particularly in answer to a battle for the Kemper business (the insurance company that, in 1983, purchased the Los Angeles-based investment banking firm of Bateman Eichler, was eventually acquired by Everen Securities in 1995, and is now part of First Union).

Reinhart had built a similar system with NIDS-based technology at Hutton, but most of big wirehouses were "doing their own thing" at this point. Merrill Lynch, for instance, decided that rather than build the required infrastructure themselves, they would encourage the money managers to build their own infrastructure so that each account, whether institutional or an individual's account, would be treated the same. This literally opened the door to APL, whose platform gave managers the unique ability to access the same data structure without corrupting each other's data, which catapulted the firm into a major player on the sponsor side. Providing this support to separate account managers tapped by Merrill became a very meaningful portion of APL's business and opened the door for smaller firms to compete with the major wirehouses.

This "win" at Kemper was much more than just a win for APL. It allowed the entire separate account business to explode from that point.

In 1984, DEC discontinued their 2060 line and by 1987, Security APL had converted to IBM mainframes. By 1991, APL adopted the UNIX platform of the IBM RS6000 series. This occurred just as Hutton announced their Select Managers program and the separate account business was really catching on. The improvements in technology had allowed account minimums to go from the institutional-sized $10 million down to $1 million, then to $500,000, then $100,000, eventually allowing individual retail clients to take advantage of institutional quality money management. Today, minimums have dropped as low as $50,000, allowing even greater retail participation in managed accounts.

As a result, Security APL foresaw the huge growth possibilities of the separate account business outside of the big wirehouses. Although its competitors were also getting involved in the space, they didn't believe the industry would go very far. While still maintaining its institutional business, APL began focusing on growing the separate account side. "UNIX was a very open architected system– it was very flexible and we were able to talk electronically to both sides of the fence, the managers and the sponsors," said Waller.

The Technology Accelerates

All of this development sprang out of the institutional side, where companies like CDA and Effron Enterprises and plan sponsor consultants like Piper Jaffray and Wilshire had developed performance reporting, universe comparisons and index data from large mainframe-based systems. Their goal was to provide proprietary consulting and technology combined.

Effron had a dial-in mainframe computer system that supplied manager data and performance reporting from a service bureau. Frontier Analytics provided institutional level asset allocation and liability modeling, and had provided most of Wilshire's software. APL was fortunate enough to come on the scene during the transition from mainframes to mini-computers and PC's, which benefited the firm greatly.

With the creation of the mini-computer and PC's, firms began developing their own performance reporting systems and outside vendors sprang up to provide other or better capabilities. Effron created a database system called Plan Sponsor Network (PSN) that was still focused on the large institutional plan sponsors. CDA sold their system to consultants, which consisted of manager data collected and input into a Lotus spreadsheet that could be manipulated. Padgette saw where the business was going and founded Mobius and its M-Search and M-Watch products, releasing in 1989 the first PC-based database that provided true manager search capabilities.

The development of the PC and later, the Internet, greatly increased the scalability of the separate account business, further enabling account minimums and fees to diminish to retail access levels. Vendors were also able to scale their services to their customers. As a case in point, when Mobius first came out with its M-Search manager database, the largest database available at the time, it included 300 managers and 900 sets of returns.

Today, the database provides information on 1,300 managers and 5,000 sets of returns, and most new data availability went from 40 days after quarter's end to one week. "This type of technology was one of the biggest contributions of the last 15-20 years [to the separate account industry]," said Padgette.

Technology continued developing and the separate account business continued to grow.

TECHNOLOGY AIDS THE INVESTMENT PROCESS FOR CONSULTANTS

Most of the major wirehouses, Merrill Lynch, UBS PaineWebber and others, had the resources to develop regional tech centers for their consultants to have access to the products available at the time – performance reporting and accounting, asset allocation and manager databases.

The "old Hutton group" continued traveling throughout the entire Hutton system, educating and training transaction-based brokers to become consultants. Consulting was a difficult "sell" at first, but they found the clients liked the concept and the consulting practice caught on quickly with them. Clients liked the approach because it was logical and analytical. But it required brokers to perform services they had never performed before and they needed efficient tools to facilitate the process.

According to Campanale, the Case system was state-of-the-art at the time because of its customization capabilities. Performance data would have to be input manually and, again, manually created spreadsheets (or bluesheets) had to be generated for each foreign account (assets custodied at other firms) and plugged in with all the other data. After this time-consuming process, such analytics as asset allocation and performance compared with specific indexes or actuarial assumptions could be performed.

Because of the technology development at Hutton, its consultants were able to offer their clients opinion-based research. Unlike their traditional institutional counterparts of the day, the broker/consultants made specific recommendations regarding which managers should be hired, why they should be hired and why they should be fired. They also were now able to provide specific analytics on portfolios each quarter, showing exactly what was going on in each portfolio and why it was happening.

Outside of the Hutton world, consultants had to develop their own systems in order to be competitive. That opened the door for companies like APL, Mobius, Effron, Frontier Analytics, CDA and PSN who catered to individual managers and their clients and later, Imaging Solutions, EMAT, and DST's entry into the separate account business.

BRINGING THE NEW TOOLS TO THE BROKER/CONSULTANTS

The first information accessible from a broker's desk was a stock quotation on a Bunker Ramo Quotron machine. Rather than follow the tape going across the front of the room, a broker could punch in a ticker symbol and receive a quote on a particular stock that was 15 to 20 minutes old. Hutton had Norman Epstein's BIPS system, which allowed brokers access to information about various products, research on particular stocks, etc. The consulting group began plugging in a database of money managers, but the BIPS system was hard to work with, making it difficult to change or update information.

To solve the problem, technical centers were set up at various locations around the country, allowing a Hutton financial consultant to send a client's bank statement to the center and, within a couple of days, present the client with complete analytics on his portfolios. Again, the business experienced a burst of growth as their financial consultants' time was freed to concentrate on attracting new business, armed with data generated by the new technology to back-up their analysis.

At the time, the technology centers had state-of-the-art hardware and software that allowed FCs to develop more sophisticated prospecting tools. After the Smart System was developed in the late 80s, the FCs also had access to a completely electronic proposal preparation tool. "They could interview clients, send the information back to Price Waterhouse, and take a complete proposal to the client, customized for his needs with specific recommendations on each detail of the portfolio. The proposal also served as a statement of investment objectives and guidelines for ERISA purposes," explained Campanale.

By this time, FCs were garnering so much new business, the technical centers couldn't turn the proposals around fast enough. The FCs wanted to provide institutional level services to their smaller retail clients, who demanded better, faster information. Today, advisors, brokers and consultants have access to the entire menu of services right from their desktops. They can generate a proposal, a performance report and all the analytics of a portfolio on demand, anytime they or a client wishes.

By the late 80s and early 90s, mutual fund wrap accounts were gaining in popularity, as mutual funds became the "hot" investment of the day. As a result, technological development on the separate account side stagnated as did separate account sales. By the mid-90s, mutual funds' popularity had begun to wane as investors and their advisors sought more customized service than funds could provide. Although technological development on the separate account side had slowed, it had not stopped, setting up the perfect scenario for a resurgence of the business as managed accounts played to the search for more customized services.

Pioneering Brokers

By the early 90s, technological development was most evident at the larger firms. Most brokers at the major firms were delivering product and consulting services to their clients using whatever the home office provided, and that varied from firm to firm, depending on each firm's resources and belief or non-belief in the separate accounts industry.

But it was the pioneer brokers who were providing more specialized services to their clients and they preferred not to wait until their firms became fully involved. Instead, they hired their own analysts, technicians and other staff, forming "small companies" within the larger firm environment and developing proprietary systems customized to serve their individual client bases.

John Brock, Senior Vice President/Investment Officer at the Brock/Hazzard Investment Group, First Union Securities, said,

"When I started in 1972 with Merrill Lynch we had Bunker-Ramo machines. They had a 4-inch tube screen and the only thing you could get was last trade and bid/asked. It was so crude it was beyond belief."

But Brock noted there was a total dearth of reporting capabilities on behalf of the firms at that time. Brock had a little hand-held calculator produced by Texas Instruments that weighed about a pound and cost around $120. He and his team would produce pie charts for clients to illustrate asset allocation (of course, that's not what they called it in those days, they were just investing in different investment areas), using an ashtray.

"We had a particular ash tray that we would use that was about four inches in diameter – it made a great little pie chart," said Brock. He would draw the circle, then take a protractor and "guess-timate" a 45% mark for one investment area, a 30% mark for another, and so on. "We would literally do that for each client. Then we progressed to a Radio Shack computer. Our first hard drive was an 8 megahertz – we thought that was really pretty fancy," he added.

"Back then, Radio Shack was one of the most advanced places you could go to get PCs," said Brock. But the computers were temperamental and always crashing, so Radio Shack had technicians on staff. Jack Hines, the technician assigned to Brock's account, became so regular at servicing the team's equipment that he eventually left, at their encouragement, and started his own consulting business. Hines has done all the team's computer work for the past 16 years.

All of this development work was self-funded. "EF Hutton was really the only firm that was doing anything in the area of managed money that was remotely organized at the top," Brock explained. "Those of us who weren't with EF Hutton had to invent our own, which, I think, gave us a tremendous head start. When you have to do it yourself, you understand the concepts better."

The newness of the separate accounts business made it difficult to gain firm compliance approval. Brock notes that management is always suspicious about brokers presenting material in other than the accepted format. So his team (which was then at Shearson) had to go through numerous compliance reviews, certifying the correctness of the formulas they used to calculate returns and making sure clients knew that the reports Brock's team produced were not an official report from the firm.

Soon after, the firm totally backtracked, fearing it had given the team too much independence, and required the inclusion of the firm's name on every report that was generated. "They didn't want us to have the independence that came from having developed independent capabilities outside of the firm's arena," said Brock.

In developing manager search capabilities, Brock and his team hired an MBA as an analyst who personally gathered ADV's from over 200 investment managers. The team did its own proprietary research manually, but used the computer to aid in its computations. Team members used their own evaluation techniques, which Brock felt was a fascinating way to learn how to separate what was important from what was not. "This industry loves to deify statistics," said Brock. "It puts too much emphasis on strings of numbers without examining what those numbers really mean."

Brock's team has invested over $750,000 over the past 15 years developing the technological tools it needs. "Everything we do in our office gets grilled with the question, 'can a machine do it?'" said Brock. "I think the computer has saved the investing public more money than it can imagine – it creates so much efficiency. What we sell people is our opinion, but how we come to that opinion is critical. That's where resources like technology come in."

Rod Hennek, Managing Director and branch manager, Morgan Keegan & Company, Inc., went through similar experiences in building his team and the technology systems to support its business. Hennek came on the scene in the mid-80s when the large firms still had regional technology centers and manager databases were crude or non-existent. "Any information you wanted about managers, you pretty much had to solicit [from your peers] and develop of your own accord," he explained.

Hennek was one of the first individual consultants to use the M-Search database by Mobius. Before that, his team would do its own research by sending out questionnaires to various managers on a regular basis, compile all the data and do all the follow-up themselves. This required hours and hours of manpower, which made the entire process painstaking and expensive.

The advent of the Association of Investment Management and Research (AIMR) performance reporting standards along with the development of the PC and the Internet forced managers to be more forthright in their reporting. It now serves as the basis for consultants to conduct comparative risk analysis and returns attribution, and to still troubleshoot the accuracy of the data

TODAY'S CHALLENGES AND POSSIBLE SOLUTIONS

Although the current technology supporting the separate account industry is vastly advanced compared to its humble beginnings, the rapid growth of the business and the massive volume that ever smaller account minimums bring are creating bottlenecks that will have to be solved – and soon.

Bob Padgette made a distinction among three sides of the business – the "front office" including manager searches, asset allocation, and investment policy; the "middle office," which includes trading and portfolio accounting, and the "back office," handling settlement, clearing, tax lot accounting and so forth. According to FRC's Keefe, the back office or operations end of the business is the area with the greatest problems. "The big players have an edge since they were in early. In the past, the front and back offices have been 'pieced' together, but many firms are looking at how to solve the problem in total, instead of having a lot of segmented pieces," he said.

To add some perspective to the situation, the mutual fund industry long has had a smoothly connected operations system that has a common protocol of its own. But that was not always the case. As funds became more popular in the late 70s, the mutual fund industry experienced a tremendous growth spurt, which caused a bottleneck of volume to occur when no infrastructure was in place to process the millions of dollars coming through the system. As those structures came into place, certain players began to dominate that part of the business because of the economies of scale created by the increased technological capability. Firms like DST dominated in the shareholder recordkeeping area, while State Street Bank and Bank of New York dominated in the custody side of the business.

Price and volume sensitivity are key, and huge economies of scale are necessary to make the processing work well. There also needs to be a common platform so the product can be sold. It may seem that these characteristics simply could be transferred to the separate account business, but things are not always be as easy as they appear. The separate account business is tremendously more complex, by its very nature as well as from a customization standpoint, and different vendors have built different systems for different purposes. The wirehouses have put together a fairly cohesive system for their particular consulting programs, and some vendors hook into these systems. But, for the most part, the industry is very fragmented in this area, an area that truly is the backbone of any future development and that is currently performed manually.

One of the problems is the lack of a common protocol or language to tie all the different systems together. According to Reinhart, "At the cottage industry stage, everybody does his own thing. But if you want to grow the business by ten to 100 times as an industry, you need standard operating procedures and protocols." Currently, administrative inefficiencies and lack of product portability are the primary obstacles to exponential growth. And instead of trending toward a common protocol, efforts to foster differentiation in the marketplace are on the rise.

One of the reasons for this, explains Erik Davidson, co-founder of Separate Account Solutions, is so firms can differentiate themselves by using platforms with unique managers and strategies, thereby offering unique value. As a separate account platform developer, he does not feel a common protocol is impending in the near future. "We're seeing firms move in the opposite direction," he said.

Reinhart pointed out that the current system creates overlap and redundancies in every tier: Front-end revenue-generating tools, supporting middleware/decision-making tools, and back-office tools. He believes a more open platform for trading executions is necessary and that trades should be pooled and executed at the firm with the best price.

The wirehouses are sort of in a world by themselves, with 80% of the players, meaning everyone outside of the wirehouses "doesn't get to play," said Gary S. Klem, former Chief Marketing and Sales Officer for EMAT. "It's like an oligopoly. 'You can only play if you play in my pool. If you play in my pool, it makes it very difficult to play in somebody else's pool.' It's a suboptimal solution – people decide not to play, and it's certainly not in the self-interest of anyone who's currently playing to change anything."

Enter DST, EMAT, CheckFree Investment Services and others. DST has been the largest provider of these services in the mutual fund world for years. Now that fund companies are scrambling to implement the separate account program, they've been asking for a similar program to handle that business and DST is looking for a way to leverage its existing products for their separate account clients. "We've been trying to use standardized interface technology wherever possible - we use FIX-based protocol on our trading interface. But we've found that there really *is* no standard for reconciliation and overnight transaction processing," said Roger Gregory, Product Manager for DST.

CheckFree, since the purchase of APL in 1996 and the subsequent purchase of Mobius, has partnered with Imaging Solutions to enhance the capabilities of both systems. By enabling the electronic capture of almost any document, Imaging Solutions gives its clients the ability to store those documents in electronic files, create interfaces that make systems like APL easier to use, and produce a seamless and much more efficient method of entering new account information — transforming CheckFree's systems into a seamless front-to-middle-to-back office process. "Areas of a company that have to act on the information, such as compliance and trading, used to have to go through a serial type process. Now, these functions can work simultaneously and reduce the time from the point of entry of the account to actual trading," said Roger S. Tausig, Imaging Solutions' President and CEO.

EMAT is the offspring of Whipple and Reinhart's efforts to

compete in the same area – operations solutions. After Whipple and Waller sold APL to CheckFree, Whipple started Osprey Partners. He joined forces with Reinhart, who founded Lockwood Financial Group and the two decided to create a complete operations outsource. Osprey took over Lockwood's entire back office, which allowed Lockwood to catapult from a $3.5 billion company to a $8.5 billion company, without operational problems, practically overnight. In the process of their collaboration, they created workflow systems for automatic—what used to be paper—processes (a.k.a. Imaging Solutions and CheckFree) and proprietary front-end development tools allowing easier broker access to separate account functions directly from the workstation.

EMAT built one central database where information as simple as names, addresses and restrictions on accounts could be posted, creating only one official record of the workflow and one central database that can inform the portfolio accounting system, the custody system, the billing system and everything that's hooked into it.

Whipple added, "We took a page out of Fedex, if you will. We created a way for brokers to take the information they have about these accounts and create even more value." Brock and Hennek agreed about the added value that technology in general is allowing them to add to their services. "Now you can check what realized or unrealized gains or losses you have, generate a performance report – give the client anything that's needed on a daily basis," said Hennek. "It gives us a competitive edge and adds value. It also helps us bring more profits to the bottom line since we control more costs now with our own systems."

Both Hennek and Brock said the real value technology has brought is having access to the information when they need it and in the form that they need it. This frees them to bring the value of their professional interpretation of the data to addressing the individual needs of their clients. "It's what you do with those numbers," said Brock, "how you interpret the data. Technology helps us look at more data more efficiently so that we can shift our focus from function to judgment."

Said Brandes' Bob Gallagher of their own technology systems that cost in the millions, "Technology is not glamorous, but it's vital. We built our platform to manage thousands of $100,000 accounts. Some firms prefer capturing the $10 million account and have the technology to service that level, but we really care about— and focus our attention on— the smaller investor so we've invested in expensive technology that allows us to do that efficiently."

A Changing Landscape

The efforts of DST, EMAT and CheckFree Investment Services to bring institutional level quality down to the retail level are developing into new technologies and redesigning the entire landscape of the separate account industry. But no one company has, to this point, solved the back-end operations problems. A key issue in the managed accounts industry is volume processing. Take billing for separate accounts, for instance. There are multiple layers and an infinite number of billing combinations that have to be considered, creating a huge problem as far as scalability is concerned.

Fees paid for clearing and custody have to be customized, as well as fees paid to money managers. Some managers are on a scale, some are on a flat fee. Said Waller, "The same type of fee customization must be done for the broker/financial consultant and each account must be accounted for—IRA's, trusts, or whatever—and whether they're charged on a bundled or unbundled basis. The process is extremely complicated. There could be 15 moving parts – are the accounts bundled, unbundled, household, etc., which is a far cry from the standard portfolio accounting system that is used outside the managed account world."

There is agreement among many of the experts in this chapter about several aspects of the separate account industry's future. Obviously, the problems associated with the back-end will have to be solved. It is generally believed that the Internet will play a large part in the solution, making system interfacing and availability of information more mobile and more accessible. The Internet has a huge role to play because many industry players have cumbersome legacy systems at nearly every point in-house.

The larger firms are beginning to provide more information

to advisors and consultants through their intranets, so the road to web-enabled capabilities is already being traveled. The journey is a long one, but the commoditization of back-end services and the adoption of a standard protocol to create a common, seamless flow from front to back end may well be inevitable.

The big mutual fund players have the most money to spend in creating these solutions. Many experts feel they will lead the way toward the change that is coming in the separate account business. The emerging affluent investor is looking toward customized managed accounts rather than mutual funds. The operations infrastructure has to be in place and there has to be a proliferation of product and advertising as in the mutual fund world.

The competition to provide seamless, total solutions is getting more heated and the process will prove to benefit the entire industry. And the ultimate benefit will be to clients. In that regard, Salomon Smith Barney's Campanale feels the future is *now.* "You want to give clients the best return and charge them a fair price for your time," he said. "That fair price is based on the amount of 'grunt work' you have to do versus actually managing the relationship with the client. If the grunt work can be taken out, and the process made increasingly quicker with more efficient technology, then everybody wins. And that's the name of the game."

Kevin Hunt, Executive Vice President Sales and Marketing for Old Mutual US Holdings, Inc. agrees with Campanale. "Looking forward, we are only going to be successful as a group if we focus on the education and the technology-- if we operate cooperatively within the industry. No one mega-manager, no one plan sponsor, will be able to solve all the issues that exist in order to really have substantial growth. We need to work in concert."

"Our particular in-dustry has to catch up with everyone else in the financial services industry."

— Paul Hatch, Chief Operating Officer
Consulting Group, Salomon Smith Barney

The technology that has been a significant catalyst in the growth of the managed accounts industry is quickly becoming a major stumbling block to further progress, many experts in the industry believe. Technological development has slowed substantially, and the separate account infrastructure has become highly fragmented.

In short, the very tool that helped to spur the rapid growth in the 70s and 80s is now taking its toll and threatens to slow the development of the entire industry at one of its most critical points. Interest in solving this situation is not the problem. Getting everyone to work together toward a solution is.

Part of the problem is the highly fragmented state of technology on the back-end operations segment. Growth and development in the separate accounts industry is happening at such an accelerated pace, critical parts of the development have been pushed back in the rush to get into the separate account space as quickly as possible.

The large wirehouse firms have been the most technologically successful so far, garnering over 70% of separate account assets. But the regional firms and independent advisor firms who use third-party platform providers are making inroads toward catching up.

Pointed out in Chapter 8, as the separate accounts industry developed, each major firm developed its own proprietary platform. Then, the regional firms and independent advisors took advantage of third-party platform providers, who began springing into action in the mid-90s. So, the major firms have different platforms as do the regional or third-party programs. As a result, a single money manager may have to deal with 50 different systems, all functioning in different ways, in order to accomplish what—outside of the separate account world—would be fairly simple tasks.

Many factors contribute to the current state of flux on the technology side. A number of firms, large as well as regional or independent, have "made do" with inefficient platforms that allow all kinds of manual intervention simply because that's what has worked up until now. Since each system still involves a good deal of manual intervention, the possibility for error is high. Ever-increasing account and transaction volumes are exacerbating the problem.

But the most blatant fragmentation in the entire managed account process clearly exists on the back end. The two stickiest points in this area are the lack of a common protocol— or language—for all platforms to use, and the tremendous volume that the now archaic systems currently in place are simply not designed to handle.

Having to work with so many different systems increases costs. Human error also increases costs. Fees are being pressured in the marketplace. Customization of individual accounts is creating even more steps in the separate account process. So far, there has been no complete solution to these problems. The industry is fast approaching make-it-or-break-it time.

FRONT-OFFICE ROADBLOCKS

Let's trace the process of what happens in a separate account, and the various obstacles that managers and sponsors face—this exercise illustrates the dysfunction throughout the industry:

- From the separate account sponsor's perspective, the main issues involve connectivity with two entities - the money managers and the trade desk. Communication with these two entities is usually manual. Since most sponsor systems are proprietary, the sponsors have to spend time and money educating their money managers on system use.

- If the managers use the sponsor's proprietary system or one that is compatible with it, trade information is automatically transferred. However, if the systems are not compatible, trade information from the manager is either faxed or e-mailed. This manual dissemination of trade information introduces one or more additional human interfaces into the process, increasing the possibility for errors.

- Some trades are still conducted through the directed broker system, in which managers agree to execute trades in the separate account through the sponsor's trade desk. However, in the interest of best execution (another aspect of separate account functionality that is coming increasingly into focus), trades can sometimes be handled "away" from the sponsor's desk. This creates even more paperwork requiring even more human intervention in transferring the information.

- Limit orders and other special trade orders are on the rise, taxing the capability of the sponsor systems even more.

- The average $1 billion asset manager has to communicate with over 20 different systems. Each system requires a separate form of communication since there is currently no standard protocol between such systems.

- The manager's system consists of a consolidated trade blotter, along with a list of trades belonging to each different account. The blotter is then separated into trades for each sponsor's proprietary system, which are then communicated over that particular system to the program sponsor. Usually the only way the manager helps to carry out best execution is by rotating orders among separate account sponsors as well as with non-SMA orders. The delays caused by the lack of interface and manual intervention cost investors money and affects their portfolio returns.

BACK-OFFICE COMPLICATIONS

Back-office operations include an even more complex set of functions. Connectivity on the back end is even more of an issue than on the front end, and it begins with the account set-up process itself. Here is the process:

- When a client decides to open an SMA account, he or she and their advisor/consultant fill out the new account forms that are very detailed. Information such as fees paid on the account, tax lot accounting, restricted stock purchases, securities being transferred "in kind" into the account, and other customization features distinguish each account in a variety of ways.

- The advisor/consultant manually enters the information on the sponsoring firm's system. The firm checks out every aspect of the account information, making sure the investment recommendations match the suitability indicated by the investor's personal financial information or investment policy statement (IPS). During this process, the account information is entered manually for the second time. Then, the information is sent either by fax or e-mail to the money manager, who enters the account information yet a third time into his proprietary system.

- There is no standardized method for transferring this account information from party to party. It can be faxed, e-mailed or downloaded using standard electronic feeds, or sent by regular mail. With the variety of information transfer methods and the multiple date re-entry points, the error rate climbs.

- Once the account is set up, authorization to begin trading the account is given. This is not the case in all situations, as some sponsors allow the manager to begin trading in the account as soon as it is set up on the system. But specific authorization is required often enough to make note. If, for some reason, a trading authorization gets overlooked, the delay can cause further hampering of returns in the account.

- After account set-up and trading resumes, the reconciliation process begins. Records of trades done in the account must be reconciled between the manager and the program sponsor. If the manager has to use a sponsor's proprietary system in addition to his own, redundancy and the lack of a standard interface result in yet more delays and opportunities for error.

- Time is also a factor in this part of the process. A conglomerate of database systems may be used to circumvent the lack of connectivity between the manager's and the sponsor's systems. This conglomerate can include databases to capture trade information, databases to reconcile the information between the two systems outside of the regular accounting system, manual data input of trades and manual reconciliation between the two systems. Any combination of these various parts can and do occur, creating even more inefficiencies in the process.

THE IDEAL SEQUENCE

In an ideal world, set-up, trading, and settlement for separate accounts would look something like this: A client wishes to open a separate account. The advisor/consultant and client meet at any location the client desires, his office, the consultant's office, the client's home – anywhere. After (or during) the interview, the initial information is input on the spot into the account set-up form on the screen.

Each subsequent meeting results in more input of the account set-up information until the form is complete. Investment guidelines, asset allocation parameters – everything the account requires including customization parameters for that particular client is completed. If the advisor/consultant tries to send incomplete or erroneous information, the process is stopped in its tracks.

The software is programmed to detect any discrepancy from missing information—something as simple as a missing zip code— to more complex issues, such as an initial account size that is lower than the manager's minimum. It will even detect suitability discrepancies, such as the submission of an aggressive growth allocation when the client's risk profile suggests low risk tolerance.

"The software would stop the process from moving to the next step," said Rorer's Bruce Aronow. "And that's part of the hang-up. If I get an account where the information's not complete, I have to check it and go back to the consultant. Maybe I reach the consultant and maybe I don't. [In the ideal situation,] you put the 'stop gap' in each part of the process."

With such stop gaps in place, making sure all the information is incorporated properly, the advisor/consultant can push a button and automatically submit the information to all interested parties. "When the account finally makes it through that process, the completed paperwork comes to me and all the other managers at the same time. It also goes to any other interested parties – custody people, compliance people, the sponsor's back office, whoever needs it," said Aronow. The managers employ their own automatic information checks and confirmation is sent that the account has been received and is in process. This is an automatic, electronic response.

The account is then sent to the trading floor, where all necessary trades are executed, simply through the push of a button. Confirmations are sent to all parties who desire them and the account is instantaneously sent through settlement, custody and reconciliation procedures. Once the account information is complete and is accepted by the sponsor's system and the managers' systems, the rest of the process happens in a matter of minutes. The account is accessible to the consultant and the client any time information on the account is needed.

That is the ideal process. Exactly when this scenario or something similar to it will become a reality depends on the forces at work in the industry, and industry participants' willingness to embrace change and facilitate the process.

NON-TECHNOLOGICAL OBSTACLES

There are other factors, not necessarily related to technology, that are causing just as many problems. Some firms are now realizing that the systems they have in place are archaic and not capable of handling the increasingly customized and massive amounts of data and functions that separate account processing requires.

Another factor affecting this situation is the catch-up activity occurring as a result of procrastination in separate account industry involvement. Firms outside of the large wirehouses are, in essence, scrambling to get on board.

New entrants that are starting from scratch in the separate account space are creating an interesting dynamic. "Incumbent firms are having their heels nipped by new entrants who are starting fresh with the new systems and don't have the baggage of legacy systems that have been in place for years," noted Lisa Harrington, Vice President of Business Development for LifeHarbor, Inc. Fee and competitive pressure is forcing these firms to do more with less in order to reclaim their margins, to be more profitable. MFS Investment Management recently installed LifeHarbor's new technology to help solve the managed account operations riddle.

Harrington cited the fragmentation of back-office solutions that have been "niche oriented to specific pieces of the value chain that product manufacturers have to offer. We don't view back-office and operations in isolation from money management or from client service."

These firms, as well as the firms having to play "catch-up," really don't know what they don't know. "It's actually quite polarized," said Harrington's colleague at LifeHarbor, Bill Poulin, Executive Vice President of Marketing. "There are incumbent firms, the old money managers, who know exactly what they're doing. They've been doing it for 20 years. Then, there's suddenly a whole new group of people just coming to the party. And those people are confused and have a lot of questions."

The issue of effective and efficient client service is another stumbling block that has arisen from the disparity of systems and platforms. The current inconsistency of procedures costs firms money, adds delays to the process, and allows more errors to occur. "There needs to be an effort towards standardization. We need to be working together on this – it can't be a situation where every sponsor sets up their own rules and expects all the managers to abide by them. That's not smart for anybody," added Aronow.

The reduction of investment management fees paid to money managers, and the pressure being put on all fronts as a result, is also a mounting concern. Money managers are increasingly more selective about the services they provide, such as training and meeting support. Travel expenses for the sales reps, administrative costs at the home office for supporting separate account business processes, and the time required for implementation are forcing managers into uncomfortable positions. They have to make difficult choices about which services to provide - services that are not as affordable as they once were.

Perhaps these problems can be addressed through the adoption of standard protocols, which would enable all systems to operate on a common communication and operational platform. This would create efficiencies regarding time, accuracy, and client service.

However, some firms are reluctant to share information and sponsor programs are inconsistent. For example, all firms perform due diligence. The firms on the sponsor side initiate the due diligence, but the money managers host the process, which from both standpoints consumes time and resources. It's also a cumbersome task.

Add the time it takes for a manager to provide due diligence information to numerous sponsor programs—each one unique and proprietary—and the costs in money and time efficiency only mount further.

A third area that currently places a stumbling block in the industry's growth is the separate account sales and marketing process itself. Widely known, one of the biggest risks in the industry today is single manager, style specific risk. "The major managed account sponsors tell us there is still a high percentage of accounts being opened with just one manager," according to Jack Sharry, President, Private Client Group at Phoenix Investment Partners. "The industry must work together and be vigilant that we don't become too 'product' oriented and drift away from the concept of providing clients a consulting process and a well-diversified portfolio."

The lack of efficiencies on the technology side, the reluctance of industry firms to share information and to work together to help the industry grow, and the resulting lack of client focus in sales and marketing efforts all contribute to the current fragmentation plaguing the separate account industry. As stated earlier, client service will be the primary beneficiary of solutions to this fragmentation.

Unrelenting pressure to lower fees means that costs must be cut and more efficient operational functions must be created to maintain the profitability of the business. The protection of margins through cost reduction and the demand for more efficient service by clients have created the need for firms to work together to ensure industry survival.

When operating solutions are achieved, sales and marketing efforts will become more client focused and will move away from the product mentality. Clients are demanding that focus. If the industry is to reach its potential, it will have to meet that demand holistically.

STANDARD PROTOCOLS, OPEN ARCHITECTURE, AND A COLLABORATIVE SPIRIT

The question remains, what exactly would a standard protocol do and how would it help create efficiencies? What other actions need to be taken that will foster the growth of this important industry, bringing greater efficiencies, more profitable businesses, and better client service to all participants?

A standard protocol "will definitely lower the barriers to entry into the marketplace," said Ian MacEachern, Senior Vice President and Director of Managed Accounts at UBS PaineWebber. "But it will also grow the whole pie because it's been a hindrance to the industry in various forms for a long time. The main benefit will be for the client. It will [create efficiencies] and remove hindrances that currently prevent clients from getting the best possible advice."

Seamless interface (which needs standard protocols in order to exist) would save sponsor firms and money managers capital, time, and frustration. In the hypothetical example cited earlier, the amount of people involved in the process would be drastically cut. The amount of paperwork would also be cut, as well as the number of errors and the money and time it costs to correct them. Sponsors and money management firms would have more time to educate consultants and their clients.

A Concerted Effort

Firms working together will benefit the entire industry. The days of competitive differentiation from a product and program standpoint are over. Value will be added through the quality of each individual consultant's advice. That advice will increase in quality through better education, smoother administrative functionality, and the ability to focus on clients' needs and objectives, rather than on selling a product, whether that product is a separate account, a multimanager account, or any other investment product.

The advancement of technology and the development of a standard protocol will benefit the industry as a whole. That development, coupled with a concerted effort by industry participants to work together to find solutions, will help to catapult the managed accounts industry to levels that are only being imagined at present.

The alternative to this desired result is a continuation of the fragmentation, inefficiencies, and profit squeeze that is now occurring, which benefits no one and may actually threaten the industry's future. Recognizing this, the Money Management Institute (MMI) is promoting closer working relationships among industry participants.

Commissioned research is highlighting the problem areas, the solutions available, and the most efficient way to implement them. Committees are attempting to bring member firms together to address those issues. According to Paul Hatch, Chief Operating Officer of the Consulting Group at Salomon Smith Barney, "Our industry [tech] has to catch up with everyone else in the financial services industry. There are entities on the institutional equity and fixed income sides where competitors and providers get together to jointly solve problems and to drive costs down. We, in the separate account business, have to work with each other in order to drive out inefficiencies and to lower the costs involved in doing the business."

The reality of dwindling fees without lower costs is laying the groundwork for a concerted effort to solve the current problems. "The only way to protect our margins is to reduce the cost of delivery, service, and operation of the business. In looking at the cost components, it becomes very clear that it is close to impossible to do that by yourself," continued Hatch.

He compared what needs to happen in the separate accounts industry to what happened in the automobile industry. Over the last 20 years, car manufacturers have recognized that in order to reduce the costs of producing a car, they have to work very closely with suppliers and distributors in order to make it all happen. In order to take advantage of technology and to get the types of efficiencies needed in the separate accounts industry, everyone needs to work together along the manufacturing chain.

Industry forces and the marketplace are providing the catalyst. MMI is providing the bridge across the competitive chasm among the competing interests. While all industry participants are dependent on each other to assure the industry's future success, there must be a mediator and a venue for the participants to work together. Hatch added, "MMI provides the platform that will allow that to happen."

Said Bob Dineen, CEO and president of Lincoln Financial Advisors, "The separate account industry continues to grow. MMI plays a very important role in the education and business initiatives of specific organizations who are aligning their practices to provide better service for their clients."

Clients will benefit from the ability of participants to offer customized separate account solutions that will not only work within the separate account or multi-manager account itself, but that will enable a client's entire portfolio to be better managed with the aid of a separate account.

As MMI and its members, and other industry organizations and firms bring down the barriers to the efficiency and service that affluent investors are demanding, the value of advice will increase. This will allow the focus to be on the entire spectrum of clients' investment goals and objectives. All in all, it will boost the effectiveness and profitability of the industry as a whole, while it fosters higher quality investment advice for clients and greater job satisfaction for those who provide it.

Resource: Deloitte and Touche

The average size of a managed account is $260,000 and the average fee is between 1.9% – 2.0%

—Research by Financial Research Corporation

10   The Evolution of Fees and the "Three Percent Solution"

With the advent of managed accounts came an entirely different and new payment structure. The original, unbundled fees came about as new services were being added to the institutional side of the business. As detailed in Chapter One, when ERISA was adopted, a whole new set of requirements was mandated for pension funds and other funds that fell under the ERISA fiduciary guidelines. The old "total trust" system was quickly replaced with such questions from clients as, "How did my portfolio perform relative to the market?" and "Are the money managers doing what they said they would do?"

These questions led to the development of component services within the managed money arena that were quite involved. Spending time with investment committees; conducting deep and lengthy discovery sessions regarding risk tolerance, the purpose of the portfolio, and what cash inflows and outflows were expected to be; researching the most appropriate managers to fulfill the portfolio's objectives within the risk parameters set; determining asset allocation and then monitoring the performance, and providing a performance report and performance attribution analysis

– all these service items were broken into separate parts and a separate fee was charged for each of them.

Institutions whose minimum account sizes were anywhere from $10 million to $100 million were very aware of trading costs through their experience. New technology allowed costs to be cut down to 10 cents and even down to six cents per share for equity trades. "So, the larger accounts would get a different fee schedule and the smaller accounts would have to pay more," said First Union's Dan Bott.

The smaller accounts were not being penalized; they were being justly charged for the trading costs relative to small accounts that could not take advantage of the economies of scale inherent in trading bigger blocks of stock. "There was a direct cost with transactions and a direct fee arrangement that compensated the consultant for the manager search, ongoing performance monitoring, ongoing asset allocation direction, etc.," Bott said. Basically, a performance report would run around $7,000, a manager search would run from $3,500 to $5,000 and asset allocation about $5,000. The total fee added together could be in the neighborhood of $17,000 per year.

THE 'THREE PERCENT SOLUTION'

The old Hutton Suggests program offered a two-part fee: one part was the manager's fee and the other part was to cover the transaction costs. The original Suggests program morphed into four versions. Suggests One and Two were fee plus commission, so the money manager charged his fee and there were commissions for transactions on top of that, according to Salomon's Frank Campanale.

Suggests Three and Four were the first programs to operate on an all-inclusive fee basis, which consisted of one fee that included the money manager and all services. Explained Campanale, "The client signed a separate document with the money manager and a separate contract with Hutton for the services. It was two different documents but everything was included in one fee. So the total fee would be "X" but the client could still see the breakdown."

He continued, "The rate of return on assets in the late 70s was approximately 5-6%. The standard compensation for a money manager at that time was 1%. Typical brokerage firm trades added up to about 3%. If 50% of the portfolio sold out and 50% was then repurchased, a non-discounted rate would be about 3%. The standard discount on institutional trades was 35%, which reduced the transaction costs to around 2%. Adding the manager fee of 1% plus the transaction fee of 2% created the all-inclusive 3% fee. That's when it became known as the "3% solution."

NEGOTIATED FEES?

After somewhat of a slow start, the 3% solution spread throughout the industry. By the mid 1980s, firms outside of Hutton began latching onto the idea quickly, following Hutton's lead, with one primary difference: they packaged managed money as a product rather than as a consulting process. Since they didn't provide much consulting, the fee they charged became subject to negotiation.

With the realization that the fees could be negotiated down fairly substantially, many firms outside of the world of Hutton began minimizing the fees to their brokers. Firms like Legg Mason, Merrill Lynch and Prudential decided to take out 25 basis points after paying the manager to cover the administrative costs. The broker would get the gross balance, taking home his percentage based on his production grid. "The fees started coming down a great deal and ever since then, firms have started to squeeze the managers [on their fees]," said Bill McVay, partner at Zephyr Associates.

From this point forward, money managers became included in brokerage firm programs on the same sub-advisory basis that Hutton initiated. There is a growing debate throughout the industry revolving around the level of fees compared with consulting services rendered.

Comparisons of fees on managed accounts have been made to the fees on mutual funds. (See chart at end of chapter provided by Lockwood Financial Services, Inc. and MMI) Some suggest that managed account fees are too high and that clients receive an equal benefit from mutual fund investing for a lower cost. However, mutual funds also net out fees before they calculate a fund's Net Asset Value (NAV), keeping the client unaware of money being taken out of the account. Therefore, especially if consulting services are included, clients receive valuable services on much smaller asset sizes than previously would have been possible, for about the same fee as a mutual fund. Also, SMA fees are negotiable and are reduced for large accounts, and this is not so for mutual funds.

This has all been made possible through technological development, which is mainly responsible for creating the greater efficiencies that spurred the development of the managed account industry. According to research firms NewRiver and FRC, the average size of a managed account is $260,000 and the average fee range is 1.9 - 2%. Their research indicates that managed account fees today are composed primarily of four parts. The money manager is paid anywhere from 30-100 basis points, depending on the size of the assets. Sponsoring firms (such as Salomon Smith Barney, Merrill Lynch, Prudential, etc.) typically receive 25 to 60 basis points. Within this fee, services such as housing the securities, trade execution and clearing or settlement functions (allocating shares to accounts, crediting payment, etc.) are included. The remainder of the fee goes to the broker or advisor/consultant. Typical compensation here ranges from 40 to 100 basis points. This part of the fee varies significantly, depending on the amount of service included by the consultant or the competition felt by the advisor selling managed money as more of a product.

FEES OF THE FUTURE

Current all-inclusive fees are between 1-1/2 – 2% and are not expected to decline much further. Advisors and consultants who provide true consulting services will be able to retain their level of fees because of the quality of service they provide.

"It's a level of service," said Campanale. "In theory, it's less service for the smaller accounts. Sometimes a client with a $500,000 account wants to talk to you every day. You might charge a client like that more than a client with ten times more money but who only wants to meet with you once a quarter or twice a year."

As technological capability increases, fees in certain areas of the process will come down. Technology creates efficiency in administrative functions for the firm as well as in the functions performed by the money manager. "[Fees] on the equity side are already being cut to 40 to 45 basis points," said McVay.

He sees those fees eventually being cut to 35 to 40 basis points on the equity side and down to 20 basis points for fixed income managers.

GENERAL FEATURES	MUTUAL FUNDS	MANAGED ACCOUNTS
Access to professional money managers	Yes	Yes
Diversified portfolio	Yes	Yes
Ability to customize portfolio	No	Yes, investors can restrict specific securities from their portfolios
Manager independence from the "herd instinct"	No, if clients want to redeem shares, fund managers must sell to raise the cash to do so	Yes, money managers can buy when the herd is selling and vice versa, customizing the decision to the client's objectives
Unlimited withdrawals/redemptions	No, most funds have restrictions	Yes
Typical account minimum	$1,000	$100,000
Access to assets	Typically next day	Three-day settlement of trades
Liquidity	Numerous	Somewhat more limited than funds
PERFORMANCE REPORTING FEATURES	MUTUAL FUNDS	MANAGED ACCOUNTS
Performance reporting	Typically semi-annual, some more frequent	Quarterly performance rating
Customized performance reporting	No, investors must calculate their own performance, which is problematic, particularly for investors who dollar cost average	Yes, automatically sent to investors every quarter, includes performance of individual portfolios and of aggregate of multiple portfolios

Charts reprinted with permission of Lockwood Financial Services, Inc. and MMI

TAX-RELATED FEATURES	MUTUAL FUNDS	MANAGED ACCOUNTS
Separately held securities	No, investor owns one security, the fund, which in turn owns a diversified portfolio	Yes, investor owns securities in an account managed by their money managers
Unrealized gains	Yes, average US mutual fund has a 20% imbedded unrealized capital gain[1]	No, cost basis of each security in this portfolio is established at time of purchase
Customized to control taxes	No, most funds are managed for pre-tax returns, and investors pay a proportionate share of taxes on capital gains	Yes, investors can instruct money managers to take gains or losses as available, to manage their tax liability
Tax-efficient handling of low cost basis stocks	No, stocks cannot be held in an investor's mutual fund account, so there is no opportunity to manage low cost basis stocks	Yes, the handling of low-cost basis stocks can be customized to the client's situation, liquidating in concert with offsetting losses, etc.
Gain/loss distribution	Virtually all gains must be distributed, losses cannot be distributed	Realized gains and losses are reported in the year recorded
COST-RELATED FEATURES	MUTUAL FUNDS	MANAGED ACCOUNTS
Expenses (excluding brokerage costs)	1.42%[1,3]	1.00%
Expenses (including brokerage costs)	1.56% average[2,3]	1.25%[3]
Volume fee discounts	No, all investors pay the same expense ratio	Yes, larger investors enjoy fee discounts
Other costs	12b-1, sales loads, redemption fees, etc.	None

1 Morningstar Principia Plus for Windows, February 2002
2 Brokerage costs estimated at 0.13%
3 Costs do not include Advisor fee, which will vary

"Everybody talks about value-added and their value proposition. What I talk to my team about is value differentiation— what differentiates you from your competition."

— R. Mark Pennington, Partner & Director
Private Advisory Services, Lord Abbett & Co.

It bears repeating: Not only are managed accounts growing in popularity, but they also are the wave of the future. As they continue to gain status and decline in cost and administration, advisors who fail to acknowledge their importance and neglect to offer them to suitable investors run the risk of losing clients and revenue. More important, managed accounts offer attractive benefits to both advisor and client.

For advisors, the immediate benefits of the managed account process are threefold:

- First, since managed accounts require an ongoing fee against assets under management, advisors provide numerous value-added services and real benefits to the client in return for this fee. A more professional relationship develops as the advisor and client together align their interests and their goals. As the assets grow, the client and the advisor can reap the rewards.

- Second, managed accounts also allow advisors to work with larger clients — like foundations and endowments and small to mid-sized institutions — that they might not otherwise have an opportunity to serve. They can also reach affluent investors, who, increasingly, want personalization and customization of their portfolios. They also want to control their exposure to taxes.

- Third, separately managed accounts allow advisors to remove themselves from the process of actually managing the money. The potential conflict of interest usually associated with transaction-based business is eliminated, and both client and advisor sit on the same side of the table. Delegating the process of managing the client's portfolio provides a greater level of professionalism and expertise.

When it comes to managed account clients, not all markets are the same. Naturally, most advisors starting out in investment management consulting begin with wealthy and high net worth individuals as a preferred group of potential clients. Many wealthy clients find managed accounts appealing because they offer benefits (such as those stated above) that make them more attractive than mutual funds. (See more about the comparisons in Chapter 10.)

Unlike mutual funds, managed accounts allow for customization that can suit the investor's needs, for example, easily comparing the holdings of a managed account with the rest of their portfolio, which can prevent over-investing in a particular sector or stock.

Tax implications of managed accounts make them more attractive than traditional mutual funds, and this is particularly important to high net worth investors. As managed account costs continue to decrease, there is no doubt that their popularity across all market segments will continue to grow.

Yet, while wealthy investors often are the most obvious market for consultants, some of the most lucrative clients in the managed account world are in the corporate world, and advisors who realize this often see their business soar beyond a traditional book of clients. Both small and mid-sized institutions present ideal opportunities for advisors and consultants who wish to move beyond individual clients. The defined benefit and contribution plans offered by the vast majority of firms require active management of the firm's and employees' assets, and skilled consultants with experience in this area can find themselves acting as liaison between a money manger and an extremely large corporate client. In addition to corporations, labor organizations and unions often provide investment opportunities to members, which are similar in nature to defined plans.

Similarly, foundations and endowments offer scenarios to prepared and knowledgeable consultants. As with institutions, both need active management of funds, yet they usually differ in asset management and tax implications because of their non-profit structure. As such, foundations and endowments are often considered a separate niche from institutions.

Family offices, in which the finances and investments from extended members of a wealthy family are pooled together, are yet another often overlooked market for consultants. This type of combined investing is common among the wealthiest families in the country, and as such, they expect active management of their investments. As with corporations, one client represents a number of investors. Yet while defined plans often address the retirement and pension needs of employees, the goals of family offices can vary from college education, to family-owned businesses, to trust funds.

All of these niche markets can be extremely lucrative for consultants looking to expand their book of business. Unlike having numerous high net worth individuals who require more frequent separate meetings, statements, and manpower, these markets demonstrate how one potential client can consist of individual investors pooled together. Each of these markets offer the potential to move away from numerous individual clients to clients of grouped investors, and doing so can increase assets under management exponentially.

Consultants looking to pursue these types of clients usually succeed by focusing on the group as one would any particular niche market. By understanding the specific needs and complexities of a niche market, the consultant is more prepared to understand and address the specific needs of a potential client. Just as financial planners often specialize in certain types of planning, a successful consultant often specializes in managing accounts for a particular type of client.

Yet consultants who decide to become niche specialists often find themselves facing stiff competition – not from other consultants, but businesses and firms also after the same market. As managed accounts encroach on mutual fund territory, fund companies are finding themselves losing market share and have begun fighting back by offering products like in-house defined contribution plans and 403(b)s for non-profit organizations.

And it's not just mutual fund companies getting in on the action. Insurance companies, banks, wirehouses, CPAs, and even online advice sites are going after a piece of the managed account market—and many are targeting the affluent. But they realize larger institutional clients bring in more assets and revenue per account than individuals, so these types of niche markets will continue to become the most competitive when attracting business.

Wells Fargo's Senior Vice President, Investment Consulting Group, Jerome Paolini, added his perspective on the widening market. "We entered the business in 1998, but there is an entire tier of banks—regional and smaller banks — that are not providing this service to their clients. Eventually they will, but banks are always slow to the party, and they are even slower to enter the business. The dilemma is how do they get into it. Through acquisition of a brokerage firm? From within their own broker/dealer? On their own bank platform since they are exempt entities from registered investment advisor registration? What is the best way?"

Continued Paolini, "Insurance companies are even slower than the banks. They have a tremendous distribution channel, but these organizations move slowly. Now many mutual fund companies are shifting over, but some have decided not to—a few of the largest fund companies won't. I also believe traditional no-load companies aren't going to do it."

ONE SIZE FITS ALL?

A leading industry researcher and expert on the affluent, Russ Prince, said, "First of all, let's be straightforward. There's a good percentage of brokers who are *not* going to be interested in doing managed account business. And that's okay. The reason is, simply, they may have grown up in the industry doing business a certain way: Selling products or just picking stocks. These advisors tend to be older and successful at their business, and their clients expect that kind of ongoing relationship. These advisors have clients who do *not* want to switch over either."

When faced with the challenge of transitioning to fee business or doing managed accounts, said Prince, an advisor needs to ask himself which clients fit this managed account solution. "Realize it's not for everyone," he said. Advisors should determine if it actually makes sense for the client and his goals. Some clients enjoy working with advisors who help them picks stocks or who provide bonds or insurance products. Perhaps this client is not ready to release control of his account to a money manager, or he is a smaller client. This individual may not be the right fit for a managed account.

Prince concluded, "After an evaluation, the advisor can then create a transition strategy for those clients to whom it does make sense. Then the advisor can build a business with new prospects, and by capturing assets from current clients."

In agreement with Prince, Mark Pennington, Partner & Director of Private Advisory Services, Lord Abbett & Co., also talked about the danger of selling managed accounts before truly understanding them. "We may be going down a very slippery slope in terms of marketing separately managed accounts as perfect for everyone," he said. "We need to delineate what the differences are between the client, consultant relationship and process versus the product attributes that owning individual securities in a separately managed account holds. The way some reporters approach it borders on being irresponsible—they are constantly trying to make product comparisons in an attempt to determine which product structure is better, for example, mutual funds or separate accounts. This depends on the clients needs. They also don't understand the value of the consultant. I like to say that 'process is personal' and everyone does and should approach this differently. But, it's important and, without the guidance of the consultant, greed and fear tend to drive the investment decision."

"If there is one word that distinguishes the intellectual history of consulting services, it is education."

— Dennis Bertrum, consulting pioneer
Chairman and Founder, Bank Street Advisors

Education. It is the backbone of the investment management consulting profession. Education took consulting from an idea to a marketing opportunity in the 70s, and from a practice in the 80s to the growing profession it is today.

In the beginning, successful consultants Lockwood, Gorman, Schilffarth and Ellis taught themselves the investment process and developed their own personal system of marketing and servicing the middle markets. Then they helped train others at Hutton through the Consulting Group, though at the time it was a rather small audience.

Hutton's Consulting Group taught brokers how to work more effectively with their clients, how to understand the consulting process, and how to market. Schilffarth believed the Group should do their own educating because they could then control the quality and accuracy of the message. Plus, it was the only game in town.

So, if a broker was outside of the Hutton inner circle, learning about consulting was achieved through informal mentorships, from successful consultants to other visionary brokers who wanted to make the transition and who were eager to learn. Those who joined the movement soon after the original circle widened were such brokers as Vic Rosasco, James Yanni, George Dunn, Tom Clark, Katie Clark, Bert Meem, Hal Rossen, Scott Thayer, Bob Rowe, and other widely respected names in our industry. These brokers-turned-consultants were admired and emulated by many, but most brokers who wanted to do this type of business soon discovered that their firms were not ready to embrace the concept, therefore limiting the type of training that was available to them.

Said Dan Bott of the early days, "Unfortunately, because there were multiple agendas out there, many brokers did not get properly trained to provide the real value they were actually capable of. They were being encouraged to sell high-revenue products, which did not necessarily build long-term good will and long-term revenue. Today, brokerage firms understand that since many of the products that had been very popular then are now being sold through multiple sales channels, their margins have come down due to competitive pricing."

Bott continued, "Therefore, fee-based revenue that's attached to the growth of the assets is very stable. Firms needed to ramp up the training and education of their entire sales force and really get behind the credibility of professional development and designations. Some firms are doing this now and it has been met with enthusiasm by their brokers."

For example, Salomon Smith Barney, known for its important views on fee-based advisory, created its Consulting Group University (CGU), in the mid 80s. The sessions were offered at a college in Michigan and were often referred to as "boot camps." This effort was one of the various initiatives offered by the Consulting Group over the years.

A big part of the fee movement and education of advisors started with Frank Campanale, president of the firm's Consulting Group division. Said Campanale, "The main goal was to teach advisors how to develop an investment strategy, and part of that was educating them on how to select money managers."

Later, in March of 1995, Len Reinhart and colleague Jim Seuffert launched the Consulting Group University (not affiliated

with Smith Barney's effort), a conference held in Texas that focused on a wide variety of consulting and managed account topics.

ICIMC AND IMCA EMERGE AS INDUSTRY FORCES

Consulting was in its infancy at this time in the 80s, so there was a
great need for an industry voice—a formal structure to help orga-
nize and legitimize the profession. Consultants realized they needed
to differentiate themselves in the crowded financial marketplace,
much like CPAs, attorneys, and CFAs do in their profession. They
wanted to take their business to a higher level, one that would
help them develop their skills and their knowledge, which, in turn,
would give them additional credibility, and a competitive advantage in their target markets. (See Chapter 11 for more information
on business development.)

Two investment consulting industry organizations were created as a result of that demand. The Investment Management Consultants Association (IMCA) was organized in 1985 and offered
advisors, brokers and money managers a platform to network and
learn more about the consulting profession. And, in 1986, the
Institute for Investment Management Consultants (IIMC) was
launched, and, in 1998, changed its name to the Institute for Certified Investment Management Consultants (ICIMC) under the
leadership of president Lewis Walker. (See more about the organizations in Chapter 5.) The two entities embraced the concept of
training and education of investment industry professionals and
promoted the importance of the investment process, which soon
began attracting high caliber brokers and financial advisors from
wirehouses to regional and independent firms across the U.S.

Shedding unproductive programs and completely revamping
its education/certification programs, ICIMC positioned itself as a
merger candidate with other similar organizations like FPA, IMCA
or NAPFA, and put itself through rigorous housecleaning. In
February 2002, ICIMC and IMCA merged to become a more
powerful professional organization for the investment consulting
community. The organizations agreed to keep the IMCA name as
well as the two designations, CIMA and CIMC.

The formation of the two initial groups served as a catalyst for those brokerage firms that realized they needed support in the areas of investment consulting and managed accounts. Educational courses, national conferences, newsletters, and regional chapter meetings all contributed to the overall professional development of advisors and brokers. High-level professional designations could be obtained through successful completion of both organizations' educational efforts.

Another avenue for those looking to fully understand the fiduciary process is The Center for Investment Training. Popularly known as the "Callan College," this widely attended educational forum provides basic to intermediate-level instruction on the investment management process. The College offers a two-and-one-half day course designed to help fiduciaries fully understand the investment management process and their role within it.

BROKERAGE FIRMS BEGIN TO OFFER TRAINING AND EDUCATION

If managed accounts stand at the gateway to bigger clients, offer more professional and customized solutions, and provide real value in terms of a proven investment process, then why aren't more firms providing training and education for their advisors?

Merrill Lynch and Prudential Securities fully understand the impact managed accounts have on their bottom line, and as such, they have addressed the issues of transitioning and training head-on.

"Managed accounts are one of the fastest growing parts of our revenue stream," said Michael J. Rice, Executive Director, Retail Branch System, Private Client Group, Prudential Securities. Although their fee-based education has existed for a few years, it was overhauled by Prudential in late 1998.

"Prior to 1998, we discussed the more technical side of fee-based and managed accounts in our training," explains Caroline Esposito, Director of Training. "But in reviewing the program and the feedback we received, we wondered why more advisors weren't moving to a fee-based business. We realized it was because they were unsure of their role in the process. It wasn't a matter of understanding the products involved, but their role essentially as a third party when dealing with these accounts. That uncertainty on their part made us realize that we needed to make some changes."

Prudential's standard training platform is called the Pyramid Program, which involves certain levels based on an advisor's needs, knowledge, and experience. "It's a pure business development program," said a Pru spokesperson, "and it does address the need for fee-based and managed money practices." With a simple and straightforward title, "Building a Fee-Based Business" is Prudential's primary educational program.

The two-day program is done completely in-house. No outside trainers are involved, although the firm's Investment Management Services Program serves as joint coordinator. The training is held in several major cities, and attendance is by invitation only, based on specific criteria such as production level and recommendations.

Coaches usually are the advisor's branch manager or regional coordinator, and they first meet two weeks after the training. Subsequent meetings follow for up to six months, addressing value theory, technical needs, and portfolio management, as well as individual problems.

While the training itself does not address the marketing needs of advisors, coaches are capable of helping in this area. But for an advisor coping with existing clients and accounts, marketing may be the last thing they think of in those first six months. Despite this, Prudential is on the right track by teaching its advisors that handling managed accounts requires a unique skill, not an arsenal of products to throw at the client.

"WHOLESALE" TRAINING FOR ADVISORS

So what does all this mean? According to FRCs Kevin Keefe, the vast majority of advisors and consultants who want training get help from outside their firm. "Fund companies are making serious inroads in the training arena," said Keefe. "The effort on training is gaining momentum and most mutual funds are providing value-added tools and custom programs, as are the separate account managers like Brandes, Rorer, and Citigroup."

In an effort to keep their funds (and their new managed account products) in front of advisors and build better relationships, firms like Putnam, American, MFS and AIM are picking up where wirehouses leave off. It's changing the way they do business, and the way they present themselves to the advisors. It's been more difficult for fund companies to sell on the finer points of SMAs, and the training—for their own sales force as well as the programs they provide advisors—is making a difference.

These visionary firms are now beginning to recognize the value of training and certification for their own internal wholesalers, or regional sales representatives. Said John Seiger, National Accounts Manager for mutual fund giant MFS in Boston, "I began to see how competitive the separately managed accounts industry was as another choice consultants could offer to their clients. When MFS launched the separate account product, the director of our Private Portfolio Services Group introduced the CIMC designation to the entire broker/dealer field force, which consists of about 48 individuals."

Understanding that a higher level of knowledge would be required to sell and promote their own products now, MFS approached their marketplace by helping their wholesalers sell a process instead of a product. Said Seiger, "In order to raise their level of credibility in the eyes of the consultants who are selling managed accounts, our sales force realized that the CIMC designation would be the perfect designation to go for. It has opened the door to a whole new world of business. The Institute has carved out a real place in the industry and it will continue to grow because it will be a place for people to go to expand their skills."

Seiger said he believed the advisors who are making the transition to more of a fee-based relationship with their client must understand the practice of consulting. "The value that an advisor brings to the table after obtaining a professional certification is in the investment process," said Seiger. "Developing the investment policy statement, delivering the asset allocation, setting goals for the long term, choosing the money managers, the constant monitoring—that's what it's all about. I think once that value is understood, the relationship with clients becomes stronger. A professional certification can help consultants do that. Plus, sales representatives who understand the entire process can relate better to these consultants and advisors, and credibility is established."

In addition to MFS, three other giants have sponsored the certification courses for their advisors, wholesalers and portfolio managers. Citigroup's Cieszko launched a significant program at Citigroup Private Asset Management and trained about 175 of their bankers (in the U.S., Hong Kong and Singapore) to do more investment consulting. Steve Gresham, Director of Sales and Marketing at Phoenix Investment Partners, enrolled 48 of his sales representatives in the program.

Said Gresham, "In the investment business, there is a bias toward the professional development designations around the portfolio development team, but comparatively speaking, there doesn't seem to be as great a focus on the professional development of the consultants who work with our financial advisors. Phoenix works with the top financial advisors in the country and overseas. So, our team needs skills in both investments and wealth management. Just as the demand for top advisors continues to increase—which raises the bar in the kinds of services they need to provide—we need to be able to do the same thing with our own people if we're going to stay relevant."

Wells Fargo introduced a group of their private bankers to professional certification courses because they put a "heavy emphasis on education and certification," said Senior VP Jerome Paolini. "We want to do this because it gives our portfolio managers a hands-on application. Our people are very good at picking stocks and handling client relationships, but they needed more insight into the investment process. The first wave we put through the course included portfolio managers in the trust area of the bank; then we helped certify about 25 of our private client managers. We consider these individuals our senior investment management consultants. It's a powerful thing to have a CIMC after your name."

Dennis Gallant, research analyst at Cerulli Associates, believes that wirehouses are stuck between a rock and a hard place. "It's hard for brokerage houses to really push for fee-based business. If brokers start feeling like they're being forced to switch, some are going to do it, but some are going to leave the firm. And the firms can't afford to lose experienced advisors. I'm not suggesting that brokerage houses shouldn't be doing more, but it's a double-edged sword."

This is where the investment consulting trade organizations fill the void. As Bott put it, "If advisors don't want to wait on the firms to provide training, then they enroll in the CIMC program, for example, and get the knowledge there."

INDEPENDENTS NEED EDUCATION, TOO

Sometimes for a firm, training isn't always so cut and dried. As a group of independent consultants, Raymond James and Associates is one such organization. They do not train advisors, so an outside educational system was created.

The Raymond James Institute of Finance (RJIF) differs from most firm training programs in one essential way: RJFS advisors can attend, but are required to pay for the education out of pocket. The idea is to keep the training completely separate from RJFS, while offering its 3,000 advisors a way to receive the education needed. The Institute provides a general education for FAs, insurance agents, and others within Raymond James' structure to create a coordinated effort. To that extent, the idea of transitioning or establishing a fee-based practice is at the advisor's discretion.

Classes taught through the Institute are presented as "problem-solving approaches" emphasizing the illustration of problems and issues and suggesting ways to solve those problems. To do that, educators come from both within Raymond James and outside teachers. The majority of teachers at the Institute are long-term RJFS advisors who've become experts on the particular problem or topic, and can explain first-hand how they've learned from their mistakes. In the case of fee accounts, they're able to give tips to advisors considering the move.

For new RJFS advisors, the requisite training program at the

Institute is the Investment Planning Module. The most encouraging aspect of the process is how the rookies are evaluated—from their first day, performance is based solely on assets under management, rather than revenue or commission. RJIF divides Raymond James' advisors into four regional areas, each of which has a major annual training conference. Classes are organized and run out of RJIF's home office and are held one weekend a month for each region.

Lockwood Financial Services launched Lockwood University in 1998, which is dedicated to money management education. Held every year, Len Reinhart and Jim Seuffert brought the concept of the training conference with them from Smith Barney's Consulting Group. The event consists of 60 sessions on such various topics as practice management, business development and technology. However, currently it is open only to those advisors and consultants who do business with Lockwood.

The firm also hosts a Strategic Partners conference every year. These events are open to advisors who make separately managed accounts the core of their independent practice. Instead of being structured as a seminar, it is more of a discussion group and networking arena.

WHAT'S THE FUTURE OF EDUCATION?

Mutual fund companies, separate account managers, private coaches and trainers, and more and more brokerage firms are all providing their own brand of fee-based or managed account training and education to advisors. E-learning or e-training is becoming popular, too, because an advisor can learn at his or her own pace, and online universities are beginning to offer specialized courses and continuing education credits. Industry trade organizations will continue to offer high level designations and professional education through conferences and study courses.

One such industry learning center (in addition to Callan College) is The Center for Fiduciary Studies, the first full-time training and research facility for investment fiduciaries. The Center, which is associated with the University of Pittsburgh Katz Graduate School of Business, provides courses on portfolio management and investment fiduciary standards of care for trustees and investment professionals "Enron and related industry scandals have made investment fiduciary responsibility front-page news," said Don Trone, director of the Center and co-author of the industry best sellers, *The Management of Investment Decisions* and *Procedural Prudence*. "The Center's courses are created to give both trustees and investment professionals practical knowledge to effectively manage the investment decision-making process."

More Advisors Obtaining Professional Designations

Even with increased competition for niche markets, advisors and consultants can stand above the crowd through professional advancement. Industry organizations that provide courses for continuing education and the earning of the professional designations as CIMC and CIMA are invaluable to advisors. In addition to the knowledge gained by earning the title, professional trade organizations assist consultants and advisors with sales and marketing issues, regulation, compliance issues, networking and support from others in the field.

"The CIMC has provided me a deeper level of understanding of the investment management process and fiduciary responsibility, as well as portfolio theory and construction," explained Damian Carroll of American Funds. "It truly gives me an edge." Carroll, who has an MBA in finance, felt the designation was necessary because of increasing competition and wanted a "tune-up" on his education. "It provides a solid theoretical background that builds confidence and provides a perspective for looking at the process of investment management deeper than you would otherwise."

Others agree that the greatest benefit of such a designation is the confidence it provides. "It puts you on a level playing field with virtually anyone you'll be talking to about investments," explained Stewart Parker, CIMC, of Citigroup Asset Management. "When you go through the program, you learn about things like discount cash flow and convexity that you probably won't talk about every day. Yet, if I do have a conversation about it, I'll certainly know what I'm talking about and can speak intelligently."

In terms of practical benefits, a CIMC designation can be of great help for individuals who have been out of school for a number of years or for those who haven't majored in finance. "This course provides valuable insight and information on the tools that are used in making determinations as to the appropriateness of different asset allocation mixes, investments, and money managers," explained Jerry Caswell, a member of ICIMC (now IMCA) for over 10 years.

But are there significant differences between the CIMC and CIMA? Not according to many familiar with both designations. "We went out of our way to see that the material covered in the CIMC curriculum overlapped virtually entirely with the curriculum of the CIMA designation," said Caswell, who sees the two as comparable designations. Caswell has dual certification with both the CIMC and CIMA, but acknowledges that the CIMC is often more practical. "Both cover the same material," he insisted, "but the CIMC program has more practical application to an advisor's practice. It's tailored for people who are working with high net worth clients, while the CIMA program is slightly more academic and quantitative."

And while some may compare such a designation to an MBA degree, those involved insist otherwise. "It's comparable to taking graduate courses in investment theory," explained Caswell. "You can begin not knowing much about investment management, but go through this material in five days, or roughly 40 hours of education and have a better understanding of consulting. I believe it's comparable to where the CFP designation was in 1980, and look how well regarded that designation is now."

In terms of marketing and competition, the designation is a distinguishing characteristic. "It puts you at a different level than the people you're competing with," Caswell offered, "which is particularly important if you're going after institutional business that's committee driven." Others, like Jim Pupillo, a past president of the former ICIMC, had more specific reasons. "I was an unproven commodity when I started in the business. I was 30 years old and needed something that would differentiate me and give the client confidence in my abilities. One way I overcame that hurdle was to get some qualifications and be able to intelligently articulate the process of what we do for clients and what the role of a consultant is. It was very critical early in my career and it still is today because it's something a lot of my competitors don't have."

Lewis Walker, CFP, CIMC, CRC and president of Atlanta-based Walker Capital Management Corporation, said that his career catapulted and his managed account business grew as a result of joining such industry organizations as the ICFP (now FPA) and the former ICIMC. "One of the best things I ever did for my business was to get involved with these organizations. As a result of networking, learning more about the profession and my desire to provide unique solutions for my clients through separate accounts and financial planning, more business followed." One of the true pioneers of the industry, Walker is a member of both organizations' boards and is a past president and chairman of the former ICFP and ICIMC.

In addition to these benefits, another advantage of the designation is the support it offers. "Investment consultants need to stay on the cutting edge of tools and concepts that are being used," claimed Carroll, "and that's what the organizations are all about – educating reps to keep them abreast of changes and ideas that they can understand and use in their own practice."

While increased competition from firms, multiple certifications, and a changing cost structure may cause some advisors to shy away from managed accounts, such activity stands to prove their growing popularity. Those who recognize these factors and appreciate the investment process will act on it, and no doubt improve their business. The clients of these advisors will recognize the value of their advice and reap the benefits as well.

So, is word of the value of the designations spreading to more advisors?

Said Lincoln Financial Advisors CEO and president Bob Dineen, "I fully expect aggregate growth within the top financial advisors at Merrill Lynch and similar firms in the separate account industry to be in the 20% plus range over the next three to five years. When you segment that growth, the top advisors who have CIMA and similar designations are growing within the 30 - 40%, versus the industry average of 25%. This increase in intellectual capital and competency is beneficial to clients as well as to the growth of the separate account business."

"The nice thing about this business," said Mariner's Bill Turchyn, "is that the people who practice it at the very high end also have a high degree of integrity. There's a great focus on the client and client objectives. If you look at groups like IMCA, FPA, MMI and other organizations, you will see that their members appreciate the education that is currently available, and take full advantage of it. I hope that as more professionals move into managed accounts, that the level of advice stays at a high quality, and advisors continue to look to higher education and more professionalism."

Higher education is exactly what Old Mutual's Kevin Hunt is espousing. "A very high percentage of [advisors] are really looking for help in wealth managment. What I would like to see is, through these organizations, the creation of some Master's Programs on a national level---a master's in Wealth Management. It would be a core curriculum at a number of major universities where advisors could get a designation. I would love to see existing organizations like IMCA be in charge of certifying candidates after graduation in that discipline as well as other disciplines on the institutional consulting side. A real designation and a real degree would go a long way toward formalizing an important body of studies. If the [industry] had a graduate program, before entering this business, advisors could participate and obtain a designation that mandated them to have continuing ed in the investment areas as well as in ethics. The end result would be better for the investor."

*"MMI will do what-
ever it takes to grow
managed accounts'
share within the over-
all financial services
marketplace."*

— Christopher Davis, Executive Director
The Money Management Institute (MMI)

13 Money Managers and Sponsors Join Forces

The industry also gave rise to another powerhouse organization, The Money Management Institute (MMI), located in Washington, DC. Before changing its name, board members and leadership in 1997, the trade association—initially founded by Citigroup's Jamie Waller—was called the St. Regis Group, then the Wrap Fee Industry Association.

The newly organized Money Management Institute took on a different shape, tone and voice. Led by Christopher Davis, a lawyer and a former assistant to President Carter, together with several key members of the industry, they created an industry force to work on behalf of sponsor firms and money mangers. One that would be a forceful advocate on behalf of the managed account industry. Len Reinhart, Frank Campanale, William Turchyn, Allen Sislen, Judy Rice and others began actively recruiting other senior executives from major Wall Street firms and their money managers.

The goals were highly targeted. First, the members of the board agreed to work together on common industry issues and concerns, and to promote members from sponsor firms as well as money management firms to "sit at the same table" to address their many challenges, and solve them in a collegial way.

Industry veteran, Peter Muratore, was appointed Chairman of the Board of Governors in late 1997. Recently retired and universally respected, Muratore brought to MMI stature and credibility enabling it to serve as neutral ground for top industry executives. Sponsor firms might have resisted a money manager as chairman and, conversely, money management firms may not have liked the idea of a brokerage firm executive in that role. But Muratore had broad experience and perspective on both sides, as well as the respect of the industry. He helped ease the members' concerns about each other, and a true spirit of camaraderie developed as he continued to remind them of what was in the best interest of the industry and, ultimately, the investor.

Early on, MMI Executive Director Davis selected several key regulatory issues to address that had been plaguing the industry. MMI sought the SEC's assistance in formalizing the regulatory regime covering managed accounts and providing "official" guidance on how the industry would operate. The mutual fund industry, perhaps sensing growing competition from the managed account sector, had maintained that the Investment Company Act of 1940 which regulates how the fund industry operates, should apply to separately managed accounts. MMI maintained the managed accounts were not "pooled" investments like mutual funds and pointed to the many operating components of a managed account that made it entirely distinctive from a fund.

REGULATORY WINS HELP MOVE INDUSTRY FORWARD

Said Davis, "MMI saw at the outset that the SEC would have to establish some kind of regulatory guidelines for how managed accounts would operate and we worked diligently with the Securities Industry Association and others to make our case with the SEC. This issue had drifted for years in Washington but, when the MMI was formed, we immediately moved it forward and, thankfully, in 1997 the SEC agreed with our request."

A year later, MMI claimed a second regulatory victory regarding trade confirmations for separately managed accounts. Since confirmations of every trade had to be sent to each separate account investor, there was numerous activity in this area and significant amounts of money spent on these tasks. MMI obtained another regulatory order from the SEC that required the trade confirms only be sent to those requesting them. The trades appear on the investors' quarterly statements anyway, and most did not want to see the individual confirms on a day-to-day basis.

These important regulatory wins demonstrated to the leaders in this sector that MMI had the "punching power" to accomplish what they couldn't do by themselves. It also fueled a rapid increase in MMI's membership. New members could see the value MMI could provide on a continual basis.

Working not only as a regulatory advocate, MMI also quickly became an advocate with the news media. "Frank Campanale, Allen Sislen and Len Reinhart suggested that our mission should be to 'end the bad rap on wrap.' Reporters didn't have reliable sources or an industry trade group to turn to. Oftentimes, industry executives would run from reporters," said Davis.

MMI stepped in as a friendly, factual voice to field questions and calls from numerous reporters and writers. Working with them to tell the positive story about separately managed accounts, the organization began providing industry data through surveys and white papers. It also explained the steps in the consulting process, fees, minimum portfolio size, customization features, and other important facts about SMAs. Once the news media began receiving accurate information from MMI reporters began writing articles that were more supportive of managed accounts. By facilitating their increased comprehension, the managed account industry received more favorable press mention.

Davis noted, "While our radar is always operating to catch inappropriate regulatory actions, MMI exists to help our members obtain and retain assets under management. Whether it's helping reporters cover our managed account sector, providing technical insights to improve how this business is conducted or bringing our members together to exchange ideas and experiences, MMI will do whatever it takes to grow managed accounts' share within the overall financial services marketplace."

The organization holds annual and regional conferences on technology, sales and marketing and operational issues. Usually entirely sold-out, the events provide a networking atmosphere and a learning environment that benefits all members. Monthly Internet meetings and conference calls for members on best practices, sales and marketing, document management, AIMR-performance reporting compliance, and other topics are another benefit the MMI provides its members.

*"Like elephants, once the herd gets going, they'll jump into it big time. The question is, **how** do they get into it?"*

— Jerome Paolini, Senior Vice President
Investment Consulting Group, Well Fargo

14 The Future of Managed Accounts and Investment Management Consulting

Assets held in separately managed accounts, which totaled about $400 billion at year-end 2001, should reach $500 billion by the end of 2002, and approach $1 trillion by 2005, according to a projection in April 2002 by Financial Research Corp. (FRC).

FRC estimated that assets under management would grow to $969 billion in 2005, $1.7 trillion in 2008, and $2.7 trillion in 2011. The number of accounts, 1.68 million at the end of 2001, is also expected to rise in 2002 to more than 2 million. Average account size, now at $260,000, is expected to decline to $244,000, an indication that SMAs are reaching a wider market and are beginning to appeal to less affluent investors.

FRC projected that new calendar year assets — actual new asset flows into managed accounts — will increase from $103.7 billion this year, to $231.9 billion in 2005, $366 billion in 2008, and $469.4 billion in 2011.

Many current mutual fund investors are candidates for managed accounts. A large percentage of their money is in defined contribution plans and will, quite possibly, roll over into managed accounts at some point. Online advice tools such as Financial Engines, mPower, FinPortfolio.com and ClearFuture will illustrate the concept of portfolio management. Tools such as SmartLeaf and Gainskeeper emphasize the importance of tax efficiency in portfolio performance. E★Trade offers separate account service direct to consumers through its Personal Money Management service.

With competition occurring within every sector, several questions arise when contemplating the future of this growing industry. What will it look like in three to five years? 10 years? Will the fee structure hold? How will consulting develop? How will technology affect that development? How should advisors and consultants plan their businesses now in order to compete down the road?

"This is and always will be a relationship business," said Jennison's John Daly. The more money a high net worth individual has, according to Daly, the more that person wants to talk with someone – and they want to talk with someone who knows what they are doing. Russ Prince of Prince and Associates agreed. "The greatest ideas or innovations in the industry won't matter unless clients find them really attractive. Separate accounts today are being seen as a stand-alone position. Well, that's fine, but as you move up in wealth, that's not going to be enough anymore."

"The broker in the 80s rarely talked about risk-adjusted performance. Today, he's not only talking about it, he's able to explain it to the client," said James G. Hesser, President, Rorer Asset Management, LLC. "As a result, we are educating folks with assets of less than $500,000 about some concepts that are helping them become longer-term investors. We've watched the influence of that on the equity markets. They're not bailing out so quickly – they're sticking with the program and the managers."

Said Peter Amendolair, former director of the Investment Consulting Group at Merrill Lynch, now retired, "I believe we will see more participants both in terms of investors, money managers and advice-givers. I don't think the fact that more individuals are entering the business is a bad thing. The competition is a good thing. We'll need to do a better job of differentiating ourselves. And the way to distinguish oneself is to provide superior advice for clients."

Others in the industry believe there will be some who will continue to do the SMA programs, while others will take the challenge and provide services in investment policy, asset allocation, manager search and monitoring. The time for customization is here.

THE BEAUTY OF CUSTOMIZATION

The ability of separate accounts to offer customization to fit an individual client's personal investment needs has been a rather dormant account feature up to now. "Right now, people are just beginning to understand and utilize the benefits of separate accounts," said FRCs Keefe. "Tax loss selling is one benefit that is very aggressively presented when the product is sold, but it doesn't seem to be a feature that's taken advantage of when the time comes."

"No question, the managed account is the wave of the future," said Bob Schulman, president and CEO of Tremont Advisors. "The term 'tax-advantaged' is a meaningful hot button to the American public and the consultant community is focusing on the money left in your pocket rather than earnings gross or net on the investment." Schulman indicated that this will bode well for the managed account business in the future.

Keefe agreed that, increasingly, investment management firms will have to accommodate more customization capabilities in order to remain competitive. "It will be more of a joint venture between client, advisor and investment manager. The manager is going to have to become a lot more flexible to accommodate and compete," he explained.

Peter Muratore also agreed that tax-advantaged investing will become increasingly important to investors. Sector investing, international investing, investing in derivatives and hedge funds are all areas where Muratore feels investors will demand specialists to handle that portion of their portfolio. All of this feeds into Prince's scenario of one, comprehensive fee encompassing a variety of customized services for the client of the future.

"We'll find," said Prince, "that managed accounts are not going to be the end of the process, but one component of a much larger process of wealth management. It's a set of different tools and processes that will fit into this bigger picture. I think the brokers at the higher end are recognizing this and are moving in that direction." The bigger picture includes such services as estate planning, retirement planning, college planning – the myriad à la carte services that exist today, bundled under an all-inclusive fee umbrella.

SMAs can morph into anything – which give them more adaptive power in the future than mutual funds. Scott Sipple, Managing Director, Regent Investment Services, said, "I believe SMAs are a product and it's sort of taboo to say that because it's been sold properly as part of a process, but, ultimately, it is a product vehicle that is used as part of that process. It's a very flexible vehicle so it can be well adapted to the investment process. The client experience is driven by what their needs are, and their needs may be broader than what a managed account can provide. At the end of the day, we can integrate it into a process that allows us to use multiple products—not just SMAs, but mutual funds and variable annuities—so that there can be a number of ways we can address the client's needs and provide a total solution."

Lockwood's Reinhart agreed. He foresees the separate account becoming a "product" rather than a "process" as it is currently viewed. "If the separately managed account business is to transition successfully from cottage industry to big business, we must abandon the institutional model and focus on the needs of individual investors," said Reinhart. He feels the most productive use of a separately managed account will be as a control account for a high net worth individual's liquid assets. This account will be used to optimize its own function as well as the function of other, less liquid, financial assets of the client.

THE SERVICE MODEL

Both Roame and Prince agreed that managed accounts will be part of a larger wealth management process. Said Roame, "The brokerage channel and the independent advisor channel are both going to the same place. The independent advisors already have the process, but they've lacked the product. They've never been able to offer stocks, bonds, separate account managers and alternative investments. The brokerage firms already had access to all the products, but they didn't really have the process. The wirehouses today are doing a fabulous job of building out the consulting process. I think that's the only way to manage your client's money."

An additional aspect of increasing the type of service that Keefe envisioned is the pruning of the number of account relationships in consultants' books. "A service environment means fewer clients with more assets, serving 100 truly affluent clients as opposed to 200 semi-affluent clients," said Keefe. The enormous amount of wealth being transferred to heirs is opening a huge window of opportunity to fuel this strategy. Keefe stressed more familial relationships, seeking the entire "cross-generational capture" as the best way for advisors and consultants to position themselves for their future in the managed accounts industry.

"There have always been firms who service family offices for the really highly affluent families, and that's how this business is developing – all the products and services are moving downstream," he said.

Bruce Aronow, Executive Vice President and Chief Financial Officer of Rorer Asset Management said, regarding his vision of the future, "You're dealing with a basket of services and you're serving the individual as closely as you can with a total package of separate accounts, mutual funds and other financial products such as annuities and others. You're dealing with an individual, not just trying to sell a product."

"It's really focusing on what the high net worth client needs," added Prudential's Janet Mariconti, "and that includes alternative investment strategies, hedge funds, trust services – really bringing all the services together, not just managed accounts. Any deliverer of services realizes all of these need to exist. I believe we are in the best place we have ever been in. We have the most knowledge and experience, and we are offering the best products and service to our clients."

Prince and Roame extend that view to the evolution of wealth management. "Advisors will become what people like to call 'wealth managers' now," said Roame. " When you think about what that means, you take a look at the four important pieces of a consumer's money. One is tax planning and preparation, two is dealing with their executive problems. The vast majority of households who reach $1 million in the country today represent either a corporate executive or a small business owner who sold his business to a corporation. So number two involves managing concentrated positions. Third is estate planning and charitable giving, and fourth is insurance products."

Roame credits these developments with the resurgence in trust services today. "The boomer generation is planning for retirement now and they have a lot more money now, so they're opening trust accounts," he said. Prince added that consulting is transforming to an advanced planning model. "It's where we talk about the whole client model and that's a generation beyond where the consulting process is at this moment," he said.

WILL IT BE A PRODUCT OR A PROCESS?

A great debate on whether managed accounts are a process or a product has surfaced along with the heightened interest in managed accounts. The interest in becoming a true consultant has its roots in the pioneers of the managed accounts industry. Of course, the managed account trend has its own mix of broker/consultants who are selling managed accounts as the latest product, but the consensus thinking seems to be that the most successful consultants will be the *true* consultants—those individuals who continually focus on providing more and more value to clients and will be compensated accordingly.

Curiously, the very evolution of the industry to that level may indeed be fueled at this juncture by a product – the Multi-Discipline Account (MDA). New product development is rampant in the industry and the barriers to entry are becoming higher every day. The proliferation of the MDA is drawing firms (*and* advisors) who are late to the party. "Yes, banks and insurance companies, as well as other investment firms, can be slow to the party," said Wells Fargo's Jerome Paolini. "But like elephants, once the herd gets going, they'll jump into it big time. The question is, *how* do they get into it?"

That is a big question, as large, well-capitalized wirehouses have the advantage of being able to buy and develop the technology and human capital needed for separately managed accounts to thrive today. "A small firm like Rorer, in 1992, would not have been able to afford to get into the business today," said Rorer's Hesser. Barriers to entry have been caused by the significantly discounted fee structure. New entrants have recently only consisted of large companies like mutual fund providers who are allowing the mutual fund business to subsidize their entrée into the separate account arena. MDAs, however, may be changing all that.

According to Citigroup's Jamie Waller, the MDA allows an investor to have access to more than one investment style within one account at a smaller account level. "Frankly, it's sweeping throughout the industry," he said. "Every wirehouse is trying to launch an MDA and every separate account manager is trying to launch an MDA." The basic idea of the MDA is to bring the diversification available to accounts consisting of $300,000 or more down to the $150,000 level. These accounts are primarily made up of two or three different style sub-accounts or "sleeves" (such as large-cap growth, large-cap value and global balanced) and are overseen by the program sponsor. "MDAs are bringing [managed account] products to a broader audience, so that certainly is going to drive the industry going forward," said FRC's Keefe.

Allen Williamson, Group President, Nuveen Managed Assets, at Nuveen/Rittenhouse and former 20-year Merrill Lynch top broker, sales manager, and sales and marketing executive for separate accounts, agreed with Keefe, "MDAs are the engine of growth for the separate account industry," said Williamson. "But a lot of people are making noise about it, and don't understand it. Savvy advisors will insist on an open architecture represented by, for example, a Fiduciary Services, or Consults, or Access where you have access to a group of 75 to 100 managers representing a culled group from a larger universe through an MDA-type platform. This offering would overlay all the investment managers, whether they are related or not, but they will be able to re-balance and customize the intervals, and look at tax efficiencies and so forth. I believe many advisors will wait for this to happen."

Paolini's concern is that many brokers are selling managed accounts as a product instead of a process. "When you have mass marketing entities plastering it and doing broad marketing, you can get everyone else in the world to sell it, but it loses its appeal as a process," he said. "Then, you begin to have this "product sale" concept applied to the business. Everyone says they're a consultant even if they sell a managed account like a product. What happens when they don't properly profile the client and the client gets disappointed because [a managed account] doesn't meet their expectations in the short term? Managed accounts are not about the short-term."

Roame cited the continuing convergence of the two. "All these products we're talking about - separate accounts, mutual funds, venture capital, hedge funds, etc. – in some cases they're the right product and in other cases they're not," said Roame. "The brokerage industry is really 'getting religion' about understanding customers and what their needs are. So, at the end of the day – and we're not there yet — you unbundle the process of consulting and that process is worth something. But after you do the consulting, you may choose to put some of the money with a money manager, some in a mutual fund, some in a hedge fund, etc. Everyone will use similar looking processes and then everyone will have different access to different products."

"It's not going to be one of these 'one-size-fits-all' models," concluded Prince, "which is the same reason why the managed accounts model itself is evolving. We're getting into a situation where what we see as 'managed accounts' today will not look the same as the 'managed accounts' of tomorrow. The higher-end advisors are realizing this, that the consulting process is built into this bigger picture that they're working with."

Barriers to Entry and the Competition

Accessibility to all the platforms and technology that are needed to properly support separately managed accounts has become extremely complex. It's expensive — so expensive that it's difficult for firms with lower capitalization to effectively enter the industry at this point. Advances in technology will help bring costs down, but that has not developed to the point of scale needed to facilitate easy entrance. Firms such as EMAT and CheckFree are building businesses providing such platforms, but the problems with back-office integration and à la carte services (as with custody and clearing) are, so far, keeping economies of scale from developing. (For more information on technology, see Chapter 8.)

However, firms that have the investable dollars to spend are finding ways to enter the fray, even at this late date. Brokerage firms are still the predominant sponsors, although banks and insurance companies are beginning to understand the value of the new market. Some workable platforms exist, but gathering the assets to support the business has been a slow process for them.

Mutual fund companies, on the other hand, have deep pockets and are already trying to recapture revenue lost from the draining of mutual fund dollars towards separate account programs. Bill Turchyn said, "Some of the larger mutual fund companies are making a move as a defensive posture. We'll see mutual fund assets migrate over to managed accounts for a whole variety of reasons, not the least of which is the tax efficiency issue, of course. A large fund complex manages many billions of dollars, so from a resource position they easily can set up the managed account capability operationally. I would welcome them as competition to the extent that the managers are talented and the clients ultimately will benefit from their work."

"The mutual funds are now having to play defense," said Gordon J. Ceresino, CEO of Harris Bretall. "They're trying to get into this business to avoid massive redemption from the shift to separately managed accounts." Competition is increasing daily, according to Ceresino. But working in the separate accounts space is different from selling mutual funds. The approach is entirely different and the jury is still out regarding whether mutual fund companies – deep pockets or not — will be able to make the transition successfully.

The same is true for the banks and insurance companies. As one advisor said, "Insurance companies sell insurance," suggesting the transition may even be more difficult for the insurance companies. Said Charles Widger, Chief Executive Officer and President of Brinker Capital, "For a large institution like an insurance company to get into the business and do it right, they'll have to invest $20-$30 million. Before they do, they need to predict the revenue stream, which is extremely difficult—especially for insurance companies and banks. The name of the game for the insurance company is life insurance, and their capital is invested in life insurance products. The management doesn't understand the technology aspect of the business. I believe many of the insurance companies that enter the business are going to seek joint venture relationships. Culturally they are very different."

One thing mutual fund companies and insurance companies have in common, though, is their vast distribution networks. Even so, the question of whether banks and insurance companies will enter the managed account world successfully remains to be seen. Will they simply acquire companies who already have separate account platforms? Many are using third-party vendors, some developed by wirehouses such as Prudential or UBS PaineWebber. The banks or insurance companies pay a fee to have the firm act as their investment management division. In return, they have all the resources available to that particular firm's brokers. Most companies seem to be testing the waters in this way before they decide to commit the dollars to developing their own platforms.

Firms like DST International, the premier name in operational systems for the mutual fund industry, are leveraging their mastery of the mutual fund industry infrastructure to build the same type of infrastructure for separate accounts. The bleeding of assets from mutual funds toward separate accounts has created a wave of fund companies that are scrambling to build separate account divisions in order to recapture lost revenues. How all of these firms will fare in the fiercely competitive environment remains to be seen. But one thing seems certain – clients will benefit from the proliferation of the consulting process.

THE ROLE OF TECHNOLOGY

Efficiency is the name of the game and the best way to gain efficiency is through better technology. The new word associated with technological efficiency is *workflow*. "I would put imaging and automation of workflow hand-in-hand," said Aronow. "They provide us with the ability to be responsive and timely."

Over the next three to five years, Aronow sees managed account sponsors beginning to explore technology more deeply. The goal is to have all paperwork on the Web, enabling a quicker and smoother interface among all facets of account set-up, trade execution, clearing and settlement functions. Workflow efficiency means greater profits.

"Technology is the enabler for everything that's happening," said Roame. "Why are we doing more of the consulting process? Because we *can*. Why are we doing more customization? Because we *can*."

Profitability of the industry is extremely price-and volume-sensitive. Huge economies of scale will be needed in the future in order to stay competitive. One chink in the armor is awkward, separated and inefficient back-end operations. Along with better technology enhancing workflow, a cohesive infrastructure must be in place for the industry to continue to thrive. "Technology is now going to start taking the next step of integrating portfolios in various locations. Financial planners have done this for a long time, but they've done it manually," said Bob Padgette. "Some of the larger firms are going to start looking at ways to do it and it's not easy. But the Internet's going to make it possible because you can move data around and a lot of interconnectivity issues will get better and better."

Brinker's Chuck Widger agreed. "Wirehouses have all the programs and they're 70 percent of the market. Their management will have to continue to invest in technology in order to make the business more efficient. You have to have the right management team and the right infra-structure," he said.

"You must have all these pieces to make the separately managed account world work," said Jay Whipple. "If you have a custody system, it's very expensive per account. Brokerage systems are very inexpensive because they're built to handle a large number of transactions, but they can't do tax lot accounting. Tax lot accounting systems are great, but they don't have the depth of security movement and cash management that brokerage systems have. So if anybody wants to have one system that does it all, they have to either start with one of these areas or they have to start from scratch. You have to tie all these systems together as seamlessly as possible."

Another area of concern is the critical role technology will play in the importance of investment style. According to performance evaluation and attribution expert, Ronald J. Surz, President of PPCA, Inc. there is plenty of room for improvement. "Let's not forget that improvements can be achieved in both areas of purported benefit – skill and diversification. Managed money programs routinely confuse style with skill, making it very difficult to deliver on the promised benefits. Styles go in and out of favor, but skill persists. If these programs are going to actually deliver superior performance, especially after taxes and fees, they're going to have to make the important distinction between style and skill."

Surz went on to explain that many sponsors search for manager talent with tools that were developed in the 1980s, before the importance of style was understood, and recognized the serious problem of confusing style with skill. Said Surz, "The sponsor has optimization technology to help him maintain diversification, but this technology generally does not incorporate style." Surz is the developer of new technology that identifies stocks by style, in a similar fashion to sector classifications.

Steve Winks, industry veteran and publisher of Senior Consultant news journal, added, "There is no question that we have breakthrough technology empowering the financial advisor to add value, that will exponentially grow the managed account business, but we have not yet pulled together as an industry to make the investment process and its associated technology accessible and user-friendly enough to cross the chasm into the mass market. In order for SMAs to grow, we must support the enabling institutions that are creating the standards, developing the technology, and providing the support that makes everything work. The SMA industry cannot operate in a one-dimensional vacuum of asset management."

FUTURE LOGISTICS

With the Internet being the "seaming" solution to workflow and tying administrative functions together in a smooth infrastructure, other logistical functions may also change to create more efficiency. "Thinking down the road, the environment will be a completely open architecture where you have not only managed accounts in a fee-based world, but every other investment known to man," said Keefe. "And ultimately, there will be a platform where you can go get any one of these regardless of the intermediary you're working with or the platform you choose."

Keefe compares this development to the old, traditional world of the high net worth individual where the trust officer at the bank not only handled the client's investments, but also paid all his bills, handled his insurance and home loans. "It's all coming downstream and technology has certainly played a role in that," added Keefe.

Outsourcing of custody functions is another way to create future efficiencies. Centralized custody determined by the money manager, according to Len Reinhart, will enable separate accounts to become portable. If a client leaves one firm, they can go to another firm and only have to change the name of the sponsor. Programs will become less expensive to build because common operating procedures will become established, enabling smaller sponsors to participate.

Aronow and Hesser feel account minimums will actually *increase*. "When you've got a $100,000 minimum, you need at least $300,000 total to get good diversification," said Hesser. Aronow added that it doesn't make sense to take a $50,000 account and place it all with a core manager. "It *does* make sense to bring in $500,000 and allot $50,000 to, say, an international manager because you don't want to allocate more than 10 percent to international, so it makes sense to the client and he's going to stay," he said.

But what happens to that $50,000 when it goes to $35,000, questioned Hesser. "Everybody can manage $50,000 or even $45,000," he said. "A typical portfolio will have at least 40 or 50 stocks, so if you get much lower than $50,000, you have to create another model. Is that really any different than the two investment processes we had in the 80s?"

Keefe concurred, "$50,000 and $75,000 minimums are probably too low – a lot of people I talk to think minimums in general will go up before they go down. Perhaps three to five years from now, you won't be able to buy a separately managed account for $50,000. Maybe it will be more like $150,000 or $200,000 per discipline and a greater total minimum in order to get the diversification you need in this type of product."

THE COMMON THREAD

The primary theme in all of these projections of the future has been the development of long-term relationships with clients and continually finding ways to provide better service. Industry organizations such as the Money Management Institute (MMI) provide senior executives better insight into trends in their business, and a platform on which key people in the industry can gather. "The MMI has been very well led. It's a wonderful, constructive force," said Widger. "When you go there, you sense what is at the heart of the business, which is integrity."

"The end game is that management firms will constantly be developing and supporting higher caliber investment people in the field. On the internal side, it's just a continuation of trying to automate this business so we can handle 140,000 accounts instead of just 40,000 accounts, all the while making every account feel just as special as the first 100 we brought through the door. That's the challenge here," said Hesser.

Bringing the valuable, personal services that have been the hallmark of building relationships with ultra high net worth individuals for decades down to accessible levels for a broader range of investors can only be a benefit. Whatever the future holds, it appears that higher quality and better service will be a magnet for assets.

"I think it's interesting to watch Wall Street make a move to a new area," said Harris Bretall's Ceresino. "In my 22 years in the business, I believe this is one of the best moves I've ever seen Wall Street make. Pricing has come down. The process puts everyone on the same side of the table. The business was founded properly, and it continues to educate and as I've watched it go through each step, it has met its challenges. I believe that if you do what is right for the client, then the outcome will *always* be right."

Michael Delfino, President and CEO, ING Managed Account Group, agreed with Ceresino and added, "The future of the SMA business is very promising. Despite the poor market performance in the early part of this decade, wealth creation over the past 21 years has been profound. Investors will need wealth management more than ever and investment consultants will provide the source of care along with asset managers and sponsor firms providing platform solutions. Service, performance and investment solutions will drive investors' success."

A Peek into the Future

In their 52-page report, *2010: A Managed Account Odyssey*, Len Reinhart and Jay Whipple discuss what is in store for the SMA business. They have taken various issues, researched and evaluated them, and included their expert opinions and recommendations.

For example, they compare the development of the managed account industry to the growth of the mutual fund industry in the 80s. The reports states that mutual fund wraps used a very similar process with only a one-product solution. The consulting process has broadened on the separate account side into a multiple-product solution set. This is a direct result of the adoption of the consulting process at the firm level. Firms will take control of the process over the next few years and separate accounts will become part of the cache of product solutions offered, including financial and estate planning.

Competition will become intense and the smaller players in the industry will either disappear or be consolidated into larger organizations. Huge investments in technology, brand identity and distribution will be required, giving larger players with deep pockets a clear advantage.

Consolidation in the industry will create huge distribution channels, not the least of which will be the large, well-established mutual fund complexes. The wirehouses have the advantage of being the first movers into the industry, which could position them very well if they can effectively create multi-channel distribution, although market share loss as a whole for the traditional firms is inevitable.

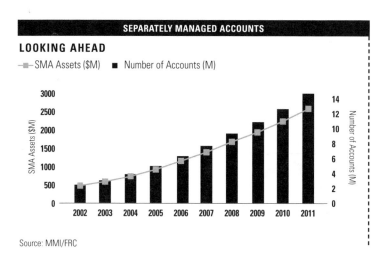

SEPARATELY MANAGED ACCOUNTS

LOOKING AHEAD

Source: MMI/FRC

Independent sponsors to the independent advisors are relatively new and the category is still ill-defined. Many such firms are under-capitalized and have had to build their infrastructures on a piecemeal basis as their asset base has grown. With intense competition looming, these firms will have to change their approach dramatically in order to survive.

Money managers will have to provide more customization services and the emergence of a "super manager" may occur for accounts in the $100,000 range. This super manager fills a new and unique niche in the industry, creating a blended portfolio of proprietary portfolio picks from a group of "parent" money manager portfolios. This simplified, lifestyle approach offers an excellent educational venue for Registered Investment Advisors (RIAs) as well as the investing public on the separate account product.

Unbundling the four major components of the separate account — the money manager, the sponsor, clearing and custody, and the advisor/consultant — will allow the separate account to offer its real value—pricing. By combining the separate compo-nents to create efficient economies of scale, the separate account will be open to exponential growth.

In their report Whipple and Reinhart also said, "We have to look at numerous scenarios, from 30% growth rates to percentage conversions from mutual funds to percentages of American wealth. The range of educated guesses for SMA assets in 2010 runs from $1.5 trillion to $5 trillion. Our conservative educated guess is $2.5 trillion by 2010."

The authors also stated that, if brought to full maturity, SMAs will take their place with mutual funds and insurance as the core products of the financial services industry. Their flexible features make them a natural choice to ride the high net worth boomer wave into retirement.

Said Reinhart, "In our willingness to innovate, in our com-mitment to quality, and in our understanding of how the world of managed money investing has already changed, we hold the keys to the future of our industry. To be one of the few big winners in 2010 will take a capital commitment to get to market quickly with a new-wave product that is scalable in its production and state-of-the-art in its value-added to the investor."

But there still are major challenges to be overcome, which is typical of industry development at this stage. A commitment to solving these challenges by the people who practice our profes-sion is the key to the industry's future.

PASSING DOWN THE LEGACY

Hilary Fiorella, Vice President of Marketing, CheckFree, said, "Within the experiences of all the very sage people—those pio-neers who we all look to—we will be able to capture their learn-ing and their experience. We can then share it with those who are new to the business and want to be successful. This is absolutely the right thing to do as we can pass along the legacy for the bet-terment of the industry."

"One of the nice things about this business," said Bill Turchyn, "is that the individuals who practice consulting at the very high end, and who have done it consistently for 20 to 25 years, have a high degree of integrity. There's no doubt the business is going to grow. I just hope it retains the level of quality and integrity it was founded on. The integrity of the investment consulting process is the core value of a managed account. This is Jim Lockwood's real legacy to us all, and it is the foundation for our industry's bright future."

Sources: Financial Research Corp. (FRC); Financial Advisor Magazine; Tiburon Research; Lockwood Financial "2010 Odyssey" Report; Financial Advisor Magazine

1950

James Lockwood joins Chicago-based brokerage firm of Straus, Bosser & McDowell in the mid-50s where he meets future partner, John Ellis.

'50

1960

The Welfare and Pension Plan Disclosure Act Amendments of 1962 gives the federal government responsibility to prevent fraud and poor administration of plan assets.

'62

Straus merges with Dempsey-Tegeler and James Lockwood becomes the largest mutual fund producer at the firm. Ellis and Lockwood team up with Tom Gorman.

'63

Harvard professor Michael C. Jensen conducts the first major study on the performance of mutual funds.

'65

| '67 | Merrill Lynch enters the performance measurement business for institutional clients. |

| '68 | AG Becker Corp. conducts the first major study of institutional plans. |

| '68 | Edwin Callan, a leader in the institutional consulting business, forms the investment measurement division of Mitchum, Jones & Templeton. |

1970

| '70 | Dempsey-Tegeler closes and Lockwood, Ellis and partner Tom Gorman join Dean Witter |

| '70 | Lockwood is the highest paid broker at Dean Witter, earning more than $1 million. |

| '70 | Butcher and Singer becomes one of the first financial services firms offering consulting services through their autonomous Butcher Consulting Group. |

| '72 | Dow closes above 1,000 for the first time. |

| '72 | Vic Rosasco joins Bache and later organizes the Senior Consulting Group after Prudential acquires Bache. He provides innovative training and support for interested brokers. |

| '73 | James Lockwood proposes new business model, but Dean Witter turns him down, rejecting Dean Witter Plus. Lockwood team approaches Hutton, and offers the concept that later becomes EF Hutton Suggests. |

Hutton forms its Consulting Group.	'73
Hutton broker John Vann opens the first SMA account for widow Hilda Peck.	'73
ERISA, the Employee Retirement Income Security Act of 1974 is enacted. Makes way for the Prudent Man Rule.	'74
Dow closes at 577 in December 1974 (45% off of its peak), its lowest level since October 1962.	'74
Hutton offers investment consulting services to retail clients.	'74
May 1, "May Day" the Big Board's fixed commission rates are abolished and brokerage commissions become negotiable.	'75
Hutton introduces Hutton Investment Management (HIM) in October.	'75
First Hutton SMA training program begins.	'76
John Calamos founds Calamos Asset Management—the first unique style manager with convertibles strategy for SMA sector.	'77
Len Reinhart joins Jim Lockwood at Hutton as analyst.	'78
Hutton sales force grows to 6,000 under the leadership of George Ball and Peter Muratore.	'79

1980

'81	Assets in Hutton's Consulting Group exceed $1 billion.
'82	Kidder Peabody creates a consulting division.
'85	IMCA launches under the guidance of Jim Owen and Dan Bott.
'85	In the mid-80s Mobius and Security APL begin offering technology solutions.
'86	Shearson Lehman Brothers launches their Portfolio Management (PM) programs.
'87	The Dow falls 508 points, or 23%, to close at 1,739 on Oct. 19, known as Black Monday.
'87	Merrill Lynch enters the managed accounts business with its Consults program.
'87	Prudential and Paine Webber test SMA waters.
'87	Hutton Select Managers program launches.
'87	Major firms establish their own trading desks for managed accounts. Jim Lockwood retires.
'88	Shearson Lehman acquires Hutton.
'88	Dan Bott launches IIMC.
'89	Shearson introduces its TRAK program, the first SMA program employing mutual funds. On January 2, the Dow Jones Industrial Average closes above 2,800.

1990

AIMR springs to life from the merger of the Financial Analysts Federation (FAF) and the Institute of Chartered Financial Analysts. (ICFA)	'90
At year-end, Shearson boasts assets totaling $4 billion.	'90
Equitable Life Assurance Society offers SMAs to investors.	'92
Shearson launches their Guided Portfolio Management (GPM) program.	'92
SEC releases the "Large Firm Report" of industry compensation practices headed by Merrill chairman Dan Tulley.	'94
Jim Lockwood passes away at age 77.	'94
An SEC commission deems compensating brokers based on client assets under management instead of by the number of trades executed a best practice by firms.	'95
On November 11, the Dow Jones Industrial Average closes for the first time above 5,000.	'95
Phoenix Investment Partners enters the SMA business.	'95
CheckFree purchases Security APL — further enhancing technology offerings.	'96
Total retail SMA assets reach $137 billion.	'97

'97	Citigroup pioneers the MDA, their own brand of multiple style portfolio.
'97	The Money Management Institute launches under the direction of Christopher Davis.
'97	Peter Muratore is elected chairman of MMI's Board of Governors.
'98	Wells Fargo enters the SMA business.
'99	March 29, the Dow Jones Industrial Average closes above 10,000.
'99	CheckFree purchases Mobius — now able to offer front, middle and back office functions.

2000

'01	Assets under managment for SMAs total $400 billion, outpacing mutual fund growth.
'02	Multi-discipline accounts become one of the fastest growing segments of the SMA industry.
'02	The Money Management Institute reports that assets held in separately managed accounts total $417 billion, at the close of second quarter, still growing amid broad market sell-offs and extreme volatility.

Key Interview Index

Key Interview Index

Key Mentions

B

Bacon, Bill 89
Blisk, Brenda 35
Blisk, David 35
Brandes, Charles 45
Buffett, Warren 73

C

Canell, George 53
Case, George 86
Chambers, Bill 35
Clark, Katie 134
Clark, Tom 35, 58, 134
Cohen, Peter 65

D

Dunn, George 134

E

Epstein, Norman 17

F

Fomon, Bob 17, 19
Frances, Bernie 53
Froebel, Carl 87, 88

G

Gepfert, John 58
Godsey, Joe 41
Goldberg, Allen 24
Griffin, Les 35

H

Hageman, Peter 36
Hayes, Sam 73

J

Jensen, Michael 6

K

Klitzberg, Richard 23
Kykendall, Larry 35

L

Levitt, Arthur 73
Lockwood, James 4, 8, 9, 11, 12, 13, 14, 15, 16, 17, 18, 19, 21, 22, 23, 25, 30, 34, 35, 40, 51, 65, 68, 69, 72, 133, 156, 169
Lotruglio, Anthony 58

M

Mason, Raymond 733
Miles, Rick 35
Miller, Alan 25
Mulvaney, Tom 35

O

O'Hara, Tom 73
Oliver, Dick 35
Owen, Jim 23, 57

P

Peck, Hilda 20
Phillips, Marty 57
Polley, Jack 58

R

Rossen, Hal 23, 134
Rowe, Bob 134
Russell, George 7

S

Schubert, Gil 16, 18
Seiger, John 138
Simmons, Hardwick 56
Suellentrop, Jim 58

Key Mentions

T

Thayer, Scott 134
Torget, Don 35
Towers, Fred 88
Tully, Dan 73

U

Ulmer, Ephraim 58

V

Vann, John 20

W

Welch, Jack 73
Whitney, Lou 14
Witter, Bill 16, 53
Wood, Bob 58

Y

Yanni, James 134

Z

Zerfoss, Carl 12

Sydney LeBlanc is a 26-year financial services industry journalist, editor, and publisher. She is currently co-director of Fisher LeBlanc Group, a financial marketing firm. As co-founder and former editor-in-chief of *Registered Representative* magazine, she also led the development of *Securities Industry Management* for branch managers. Sydney was involved in the formative stages of the Institute for

Certified Investment Management Consultants in the mid-1980s. She was senior editor and partner with horsesmouth.com, an e-learning and training site for brokers, and a senior writer and columnist for Morningstaradvisor.com.

Currently a consulting editor for *Senior Consultant News Journal* and editor of "Managed Accounts Quarterly" in *Financial Advisor,* Sydney is co-author of *Streetwise Investor, Little Known Facts from Wall Street,* and *PR Savvy for the Financial Professional.* She is the recipient of several awards for her work, including the *FOLIO* Editorial Excellence Award for *Securities Industry Management,* and First Place for Signed Editorial from the American Society of Business Press Editors.